Hitchh

www.pocketessentials.com

Also by M.J. Simpson
Hitchhiker: A Biography of Douglas Adams

Hitchhiker's Guide

M.J. Simpson

Completely and
Utterly Unauthorised

www.pocketessentials.com

This edition published in 2005 by Pocket Essentials
P.O.Box 394, Harpenden, Herts, AL5 1XJ
www.pocketessentials.com

Distributed in the USA by Trafalgar Square Publishing, P.O. Box 257, Howe Hill
Road, North Pomfret, Vermont 05053

A CIP catalogue record for this book is available from the British Library.

ISBN 1 904048 46 3

2 4 6 8 10 9 7 5 3 1

Typeset by Avocet, Typeset, Chilton, Aylesbury, Bucks
Printed and bound in Great Britain by Cox & Wyman, Reading

In memory of Peter Jones, Douglas Adams
and Dr Harry Porter

Acknowledgements

In preparing this book, I have been assisted by many
people, to whom my thanks are extended: Will Adams,
Sophie Astin, Martin Benson, Rayner Bourton, Simon
Brett, Jonathan Cecil, Mike Cule, Kevin Jon Davies, Paul
Duncan, the late Jim Francis, Neil Gaiman, Dave Golder,
Stephen Grief, Richard Hollis, Roy Hudd, the late Peter
Jones, Simon Jones, Lizzy Kremer, Geoff McGivern, Dirk
Maggs, Joe Melia, Ion Mills, Stephen Moore, Stan
Nicholls, Geoffrey Perkins, Andrew Pixley, Terry Platt,
Liam Proven, Dave Prowse, Susan Sheridan, Michael
Marshall Smith, Aubrey Woods, Matt Zimmerman and –
without whom, etc. – Douglas Adams. Apologies if I have
missed anyone out.

This book would also not have been possible without
the long-term support and encouragement of my parents,
without the forbearance and understanding of my wife
Hillary, or without the assistance of a small, furry creature
from Alpha Centauri.

Contents

CONTENTS

Foreword by Simon Jones

It's always been a bit of a mystery to me. My old friend Douglas Adams has always maintained that he wrote the character of Arthur Dent, hero/victim of *The Hitchhiker's Guide to the Galaxy*, with me in mind. Personally I've never seen the resemblance. To be brutally frank, he didn't seem anything like me. I mean, Arthur is a man who spends much of his time touring the universe in a dressing gown, in a state of bewilderment bordering on irritability, complaining much of the time about the absence of a really good cup of tea. The irritability stems not just from his state of physical dislocation, but also from a vague sense of unease that nothing is quite what it seems, and never has been. He's easily distracted by trivia, and he keeps thinking it's Thursday.

Actually I think it was a Thursday when I heard from this fellow Mike Simpson. He was in England, and I was in New York, so for me it was a good bit earlier in the morning than it was for him. In fact, I'd just got out of bed and put the kettle on.

He came straight to the point. "How would you like to write a foreword to my book about *The Hitchhiker's Guide*?"

Of course, my suspicions were immediately aroused.

"What book? What's it about?"

He replied that it was a complete chronology of all the versions in the media of Douglas' classic work. He added, "You know – all the details of your life as Arthur Dent."

I gave it some thought. Put that way, it sounded really quite interesting, but nonetheless I felt it my duty to wonder aloud, "Is this really something the world needs?"

His reply struck me as a bit sharp in tone. "Yes, it is, or I wouldn't have written it."

"Oh ho!" I thought, "Someone got out of bed the wrong side – and it wasn't me." Actually I can't get out of bed the wrong side, because my wife sleeps on the other – unless I've been on the wrong side all this time and never known it …

I leave him on hold because the kettle has boiled by now, and I have to warm the pot before letting the tea infuse or it'll be undrinkable. As I pour the water on the leaves – while it's boiling, or it's a waste of time – I think about his proposition. He has a point. The world does need this book. I need this book. Once and for all I could prove to people that the radio series came before the books – something a surprising number of people don't know and wilfully won't believe when I tell them. A definitive where-and-when sort of book would settle all sorts of pointless and time-wasting debates. It astonishes me what far-fetched theories are floating out there in the ether. Someone once told me that The Who had planned a rock opera with Roger Daltry as Arthur and Pete Townsend as The Book – crazy of course, but sort of intriguing. Who was it who came up with the idea that there was a nine-hour experimental German film directed by a disciple of Rainer Werner Fassbinder that's lying forgotten in a deserted cellar in Leipzig? Or did I dream that one?

While I was waiting for the tea to steep, I heard a squawking from the telephone. Mike Simpson was becoming impatient. "Well?" he said, "Will you do it?" He seemed to be in rather a hurry. "Look – I can e-mail you the book if you want to look at it first."

"No, no, don't trouble … or well, maybe, yes, do."

Oh, the Information Superhighway! I've no idea how it works but it still gives me a thrill.

I waited – not very long – and there it was, available to download. Of course that was easier said than done – but after a struggle during which I became convinced that I'd consigned the whole file to oblivion, I had it on the screen and, soon after that, printed out. So I read it – and found it very comprehensive, accurate and intriguing. My name's mentioned a lot, and for some reason I find that comforting, although I'm not very thrilled to read that I'm too old to play Arthur in the Hollywood movie version. Not enough of a box-office name, I suspect. But if I am too old, it's because I've had to wait too long for it. The eventual cast, if you want my opinion, hasn't even been born yet …

Anyway, I called him back. I congratulated him on his scholarship, and told him I'd be delighted, nay, honoured, to write some sort of foreword – though I wasn't at all sure what I could think of to say. I'd just put down the receiver when I remembered the tea. It had stewed to the colour and consistency of prune juice – a complete waste of prime second flush Assam, which isn't at all easy to come by.

Oh, this book? It's great. Read and enjoy. (Now, where have I heard that before?)

Simon Jones
New York, November 2000

Foreword to the 2005 edition

Oh dear. Reading over my foreword to the first edition is like looking at a photograph taken at Ascot in the balmy summer of 1914. Those top-hatted men and elegantly-stayed ladies had no idea what was about to befall them, just as I had no inkling of what lay ahead for me, for Arthur Dent, and for Douglas. We couldn't be expected to guess how the cards might fall – but we weren't prepared for what did take place even in our wildest imaginings.

2001 was a year that changed everything, with brutal suddenness. But for those of us connected in our various ways to *The Hitchhiker's Guide to the Galaxy*, from fans to cast, the real disaster took place in May, well before the general cataclysm of 11 September, when Douglas succumbed to a massive and entirely unexpected heart attack during a routine session of weightlifting at his local gym in Santa Barbara.

We were all devastated, though none so much as his family, his wife Jane and daughter Polly. The reaction on the Internet was remarkable; there was an enormous outpouring of grief from all the corners of the Earth – a phenomenon that would surely have astonished Douglas himself. It was apparently a coincidence, but it seemed wonderfully apt that, at his funeral in California, we were able to announce that the official entity that does such things had just named a distant astral body after Arthur Dent. It also seemed inevitable that, when I sadly glanced at my boarding card on the flight back to New York after the ceremony, I found I was flying on Delta Flight 42. (I'm not making this up. I still have the card.)

I was not in New York on 9:11; I was in London for Douglas' Memorial at Saint Martin-in-the-Fields, but I couldn't forget the time nearly 18 years before when we dined at Windows on the World, the restaurant at the top of the World Trade Center. Douglas had announced that he was driving from the West Coast and he wanted to have dinner there. Would we book? It turned out that Terry Gilliam was flying in from Canada that same day, and so we arranged to meet there at the tower's top floor. It seemed to me that the moment was sufficiently auspicious for me to take my courage in both hands and propose to my girlfriend, Nancy Lewis, the American manager of Monty Python, who had been a friend of Douglas before she and I had met each other. So I dropped to my knee on the floor of one of the last spacious checker cabs in Manhattan, and she graciously accepted. We arrived in exultant mood at the restaurant, only to be greeted by the *maitre d'* who was most apologetic, explaining that the fire alarm had been accidentally triggered, causing the kitchen to be covered in green foam. Appalled, we explained to him the significance of the occasion, and with further apologies he gave us a bottle of champagne and directed us to the neighbouring sushi bar. In due course the others arrived, and their disappointment at the loss of a gourmet evening was, we hoped, mitigated by our celebration. There in London, I reflected on the horrifying destruction and loss of life, and, as a passing thought, pondered that not only would Douglas now never dine there, but nor would anyone else.

But there at Saint Martin-in-the-Fields, the radio producer, Dirk Maggs, met with Bruce Hyman, whose company, Above the Title, had been responsible for a string of distinguished programmes for the BBC. Back in 1994, there had nearly been another series following on from the Secondary Phase. Dirk had actually booked us all to reprise our characters, but the effort foundered because Douglas was unhappy with the scripts. We were all paid – but we would rather have made the programmes. As it was, by the time of Douglas' death, the prospect, as far as I could see, of recording the remaining three books had entirely disappeared. Peter Jones, David Tate and Richard Vernon had all left us – it seemed hardly worth the effort. But Bruce and Dirk were determined to see it through, as a tribute to Douglas.

So it was that in November 2003 the surviving original cast assembled at the Sound House Recording Studios to compare hairlines – I lost – and to slip back into the old roles, which we found fitted like old comfy gloves. That was *Life, the Universe and Everything* aka *The Tertiary Phase*. Now, in January 2005, we've laid down *So Long, and Thanks for All the Fish* and *Mostly Harmless*. I'll admit that finishing the job was strangely important to me, but the sense of a completed mission is tempered by a reluctant admission that I may have said my last lines as Arthur Dent. He and I have been joined at the hip for more than twenty-five years, and I suppose we'll always be inextricably linked.

In the week following the last studio session, I had three other engagements – all of which bore the traces of Douglas. On the Monday and Tuesday, I recorded an audio book of Noel Coward short stories for Harper Audio at Motivation Studios, near Finchley Road Tube Station. I had barely been there a few minutes before I learnt that it was there that Douglas had recorded all the *Hitchhiker* books. On the Wednesday, I appeared in a BBC Radio drama – Episode Four of *The League of Queer Trades* by GK Chesterton. Who should be in the cast (apart from Geoff McGivern, through whose good offices I was there) but Martin Freeman, who has assumed the role of Arthur Dent in the Touchstone movie? The chances of our meeting so soon had to be rather remote, but I can report that we chatted amiably enough, and while I'm not passing on any torches or batons, I wish him the best of luck. On Thursday, I was interviewed by an outfit called Objective TV for a programme about landmark shows of the eighties, to discuss *Hitchhiker's* and *Brideshead Revisited*. Douglas, it seems, is not going to leave me alone, and I'm delighted to do all I can to promote his witty work.

Mike Simpson, it's fair to say, has done more than anyone to keep the flame of *H2G2* alive over the years with his enthusiasm and unflagging support. As I said of his excellent biography of Douglas, *Hitchhiker*: 'It was generally remarked, even by his subject, that Simpson knew more about Adams than Adams himself.' It remains true to this day and for any enthusiast of the Adams *oeuvre*, this little guide is not only entertaining, but impeccably comprehensive and most certainly 'essential'.

Simon Jones London, January 2005

1: Introduction

Where to begin?

The Hitchhiker's Guide to the Galaxy does not follow any sort of pattern. It does not, for example, have any preferred medium. It has been equally successful on radio, on television, on record, as novels, as talking books, on stage, as a computer game and most recently as a feature film. All these different versions tell roughly the same story, but not necessarily in the same way. And on numerous occasions they flatly contradict each other.

This does not make it an easy subject to write a book about. Far from it.

There is no logical progression to be had here: no episode guide, no filmography, not even a clearly defined chronological progression. What there is instead is a genuine multimedia phenomenon – a global success without precedent or parallel. Or, unfortunately, order. I have done my best to make sense of it.

Surprisingly, there has been relatively little attempt to document this phenomenon (with the obvious exception of Neil Gaiman's book *Don't Panic*, which I had the honour of revising and updating for its third edition in 2002), although two biographies of the *Hitchhiker's Guide*'s creator Douglas Adams have been published since his death in 2001. It is hoped that this book will go some way to explaining and charting this incredible story, and the incredible story behind it.

So where to begin?

Half past ten on Wednesday 8 March 1978 is as good a place as any to begin the story of *The Hitchhiker's Guide to the Galaxy*. In those days, the BBC still made a lot of radio comedy, almost invariably written and performed by Oxbridge graduates (the 'alternative comedy' scene was still struggling to find its own identity in a London strip club). Regular listeners to Radio 4 knew to check the *Radio Times* each week, examining certain broadcast slots – 12.27pm, 6.30pm, 10.30pm – for the latest offerings from the Light Entertainment Department at Broadcasting House.

That initial listing for *The Hitchhiker's Guide to the Galaxy* gave no indication that it was to be any different from any of the series before, after, or running concurrently. There was a recognisable name in the cast – Peter Jones, rather mysteriously credited as 'The Book' – and radio comedy obsessives may have recognised writer Douglas Adams' name from occasional credits on *The News Huddlines*. The episode title, 'Fit the First', would have seemed a mere whim to most, although fans of Lewis Carroll may have recognised a reference to *The Hunting of the Snark*. (The Milliways restaurant slogan 'If you've believed six impossible things before breakfast this morning ...' was another Carroll reference, although the existence of a 'rule 42' in *Through the Looking Glass* was mere coincidence, according to Adams.) Nevertheless, there was no clue as to quite how different this new series was going to be.

For one thing, it did not have an audience. Radio 4 policy was clear: if you were a comedy series, whether sitcom, revue or variety, you had to have an audience. Yet the listeners on that March evening, in their bedsits and their baths, found themselves laughing aloud and alone – which, given the solitary nature of the typical late-night Radio 4 listener, was not as embarrassing as it might have been.

The show was an instant hit, on a scale unseen since the golden age of radio in the 1950s. It very rapidly established itself as worthy of being mentioned in the same breath as radio classics like *Hancock's Half Hour*, *The Goon Show* and *I'm Sorry, I'll Read That Again*.

Real, hardcore, purist *Hitchhiker's Guide* fans still consider the original six-part radio series to be the definitive version of the story. But *The Hitchhiker's Guide to the Galaxy* has a popularity that extends way beyond its hardcore fans, and its numerous incarnations mean that it is something different to different people.

To some it is a cult radio series, to others an early 1980s TV comedy, to others a series of best-selling science fiction novels – and to some people it is now a Hollywood movie. Ironically, Douglas Adams never set out to be either a science fiction writer or a novelist.

If one is to trace the origins of *Hitchhiker's Guide*, one has to look at the Footlights Society, that elitist yet prolific group of ever-changing Cambridge undergraduates which has been producing great names in comedy for over a century. The casts of *Monty Python's Flying Circus*, *The Goodies* and *Beyond the Fringe* were wholly or partly composed of Footlights alumni, and the Footlights influence is as strong in *Hitchhiker's* as in any of those other shows. Douglas Adams attended Cambridge University in the early 1970s and there met Simon Jones, Mark Wing-Davey and Geoffrey McGivern, who were to be the inspirations for the characters they were later to play.

Pinning down just why *The Hitchhiker's Guide to the Galaxy* has been so successful is an impossible task, but there is one very obvious way in which it was truly groundbreaking. It was the first genuinely successful attempt to combine science fiction with comedy. Which is not to say that there had not previously been humorous science fiction, but the works of writers like Harry Harrison or Robert Sheckley were spoofs of the genre, written by and for people familiar with science fiction's conventions and intricacies. They were humorous science fiction, as opposed to science fiction humour.

Attempts at injecting science fiction into more populist comedy were more problematical. American TV producers had managed it briefly with the 1960s sitcom *My Favorite Martian*, but this was simply a strictly Earth-bound fish-out-of-water fantasy along the lines of *I Dream of Jeannie* or *Bewitched*. The BBC's misguided attempts at this blending of genres resulted in the infamously dire *Come Back Mrs Noah*, starring Molly Sugden (broadcast after *Hitchhiker's Guide's* radio debut, but shown as a pilot before it). It was to be another decade before they got it right again with *Red Dwarf*.

Where Douglas Adams succeeded was in writing a story which was actually a satire on human existence and foibles, just blown up to a galactic scale. In that respect his predecessors were people like Jonathan Swift, whose

Gulliver's Travels ploughed a similar furrow. Adams always maintained that he didn't set out to write a science fiction series, but after blowing up the world in the first episode, he was left with no other choice.

One of the reasons for the series' initial success was undoubtedly the science fiction fever which gripped the UK, and indeed the world, in the late 1970s, fuelled by the massive success of *Star Wars*. George Lucas' film, which had created a media craving for anything to do with spaceships, aliens or robots, very fortuitously opened across the UK in January 1978, less than six weeks before *Hitchhiker's* debuted. However, the BBC commissioned Adams to write 'Fit the First' in March 1977, before *Star Wars* even opened in America, and certainly before the sci-fi hype began.

Despite his best efforts to deny the label, Douglas Adams became irrevocably branded as a science fiction author, and a spectacularly successful one at that, whose books could command enormous advances. He was also an almost evangelical advocate of new technology, from his early experiments with computers that produced, for example, the distorted self-portrait on the cover of *The Hitchhiker's Guide to the Galaxy: The Original Radio Scripts*, to his later directorship of h2g2 (aka The Digital Village) and his position as one of the most sought-after speakers for technology conferences.

But above all this, above and beyond the success of *Hitchhiker's Guide*, the state-of-the-art Apple Macintoshes, the world's largest collection of left-handed guitars and the endless globe-trotting, one thing asserts itself time and again as one reads this book and follows the story of Douglas Adams' success.

He never got the hang of deadlines.

Everybody who ever worked with Douglas Adams encountered this problem, and tales are legion of the author being locked in hotel rooms to finish novels or scribbling last-minute changes to scripts on toilet paper. Not all of these stories are apocryphal. Even more incredibly, this inability to make deadlines seemed to be transferable and affected even aspects of the *Hitchhiker's Guide* canon with which Adams himself was not directly involved. Publicists around the globe threw their hands up in horror when presented with a new Douglas Adams project because there was no way of knowing when, if ever, it would appear.

Fortunately, Douglas Adams was actually not very prolific. As an author, he published only seven novels in 21 years, of which two were largely derived from radio scripts, and two were based on *Doctor Who* stories. Never afraid to reformat material into new media, Adams had something of a reputation for recycling, which became a running joke among his friends.

Many ideas from *Hitchhiker's Guide* have become common cultural currency in the past two decades, notably phrases such as 'life, don't talk to me about life' and 'large, friendly letters,' but the most celebrated element of the entire *Hitchhiker's* saga is the idea that there is a single, definitive answer to all the questions of the universe, and that it is the number 42. More than any other aspect of the story, the significance of 42 and the phrase which pre-empted it, 'life, the universe and everything' have become enshrined in the cultural zeitgeist of the late twentieth century (and now the twenty-first).

Scientists have for many years been searching for a single, unifying theory of everything, and consequently *Hitchhiker's Guide* and its central joke have always been enormously popular among the scientific community. Even Arthur C Clarke referred to 42 as the meaning of life in his novel *Rama Revealed*. In fact, the idea that a single number may lie at the heart of all science is not inconceivable, given the range of factors which have a constant numerical value. *Pi*, *e*, *c* and the Avogadro constant are just four examples of numerical absolutes liable to be encountered by students of maths or physics, although none of them, admittedly, is a nice, round integer like 42.

Adams claimed that he picked 42 because it was 'the most humorous of the two-figure numbers' and undoubtedly got fed up with questions from fans, some of whom seemed to think that the number had genuine (probably hilarious) significance but just needed to be explained a wee bit more. An audible groan could be heard at Adams' talks whenever someone (usually, it must be said, an American) asked him why he chose 42, presumably believing that (a) he had not been asked this before, or (b) his previous explanations had somehow passed the questioner by.

There are many coincidental appearances of 42 in literature, the media and the world, some of which (if created after 1978) may be in deliberate homage to *Hitchhiker's Guide*. However, most occurrences of the number are merely coincidental, and not particularly interesting coincidences at that. In any corner shop or supermarket there will be items which cost 42p, in any reasonably sized street there will be a house number 42. Every individual encounters scores of two-figure numbers every day, and on a purely statistical level, approximately one per cent of those are likely to be 42. (In fact, since smaller numbers are commoner – they occur in both small groups and large groups – and 42 lies in the bottom half of the range 1–99, it will likely account for slightly more than one per cent.)

There is no special significance to 42. That, in fact, is precisely what makes the joke so funny.

Clear proof of 42's ordinariness lies in the fact that other two-figure numbers have just as much significance to other groups of fans. Readers of Robert Anton Wilson and Robert Shea's *Illuminatus Trilogy*, for example, know the importance of 23 and how frequently it occurs, while fans of American musical japester 'Weird Al' Yankovic watch out for occurrences of 27 and find them just as often. It is obvious that Douglas Adams could have picked any reasonably sized number for Deep Thought's answer and it would have been discovered to crop up elsewhere on a frequent basis. The one and only significance to 42 is that (in English, at least) it sounds amusing with its 'or,' 'ee' and 'oo' sounds. That's it. That is the sum total significance of 42. It's a funny-sounding number.

The storyline of *The Hitchhiker's Guide to the Galaxy* is complex, contradictory and unfailingly bizarre, full of inexplicable events and bizarre characters. The story behind *The Hitchhiker's Guide to the Galaxy* is just as complex, contradictory and bizarre, and is equally full of inexplicable events and bizarre characters. The one perfectly complements the other. This book is an attempt to tell this latter story, based on extensive research and numerous interviews.

The first edition of this book was published in April 2001. Less than a month later, Douglas Adams suffered a massive, unexpected heart attack in a Californian gym and passed away at the appallingly early age of 49. I have been told that the copy which I sent to him was found on his desk. A second edition with a new afterword was published later that year. For this new edition the entire text has been substantially revised, taking into account not only Adams' death but also the flurry of *Hitchhiker's Guide* activity since then.

Where then, should we actually begin?

Why not begin on a rock on the North side of Santorini in 1974, where 22-year-old Douglas Adams is lying exhausted but happy, under a starry sky and alongside a young lady from Holland? He picks up his well-thumbed copy of the essential undergraduate travel book, *A Hitchhiker's Guide to Europe*, and wonders whether somebody could write a similar volume for interstellar travellers – *The Hitchhiker's Guide to the Galaxy*.

That was more than thirty years ago …

M.J. Simpson
Leicester, October 2000 and February 2004

Feedback on this book is positively encouraged, and may be sent c/o Pocket Essentials, or directly to pocket@planetmagrathea.com

2. The Radio Series

The Primary Phase

Fit the First:
First broadcast: 8 March 1978

Cast: Peter Jones, Simon Jones, Geoffrey McGivern, Bill Wallis, Jo Kendall, David Gooderson

Story: Arthur Dent wakes up one morning to discover that his house is about to be knocked down to make way for a bypass. Before this can happen, he discovers that his friend Ford Prefect is an alien and that the entire Earth is about to be demolished to make way for a hyperspace bypass.

Ford is a travelling researcher for an electronic guide-book, *The Hitchhiker's Guide to the Galaxy*, and successfully transports himself and Arthur onto the Vogon ship moments before it destroys the planet. Arthur is given a Babel Fish in his ear to help him understand alien languages and a towel for everything else. Unfortunately, the Vogons have detected their arrival on the ship and the Vogon captain tortures them with some of his poetry.

Fit the Second:
First broadcast: 15 March 1978

Cast: Peter Jones, Simon Jones, Geoffrey McGivern, Bill Wallis, David Tate, Susan Sheridan, Mark Wing-Davey, Stephen Moore

Story: After unsuccessfully attempting to flatter the Vogon Captain, Arthur and Ford are thrown off the ship but are unexpectedly picked up by the *Heart of Gold*, a spaceship powered by the Infinite Improbability Drive. Improbable as it may seem, the stolen spaceship is under the command of Zaphod Beeblebrox, part-time Galactic President and a distant relative of Ford's, accompanied by his human girlfriend, Tricia 'Trillian' McMillan. Zaphod met Trillian at a party in Islington where she was being chatted up by Arthur. The ship is also equipped with an overly cheerful computer named Eddie and a manically depressed robot called Marvin.

Fit the Third:
First broadcast: 22 March 1978

Cast: Peter Jones, Simon Jones, Geoffrey McGivern, David Tate, Susan Sheridan, Mark Wing-Davey, Stephen Moore, Richard Vernon

Story: The *Heart of Gold* orbits the legendary planet Magrathea, once the home of a custom planet-building industry. Two automated guided missiles aimed at the ship are rendered harmless when Arthur turns on the Infinite

Improbability Drive. In the chaos, Trillian's two pet mice escape.

Landing on the planet, Zaphod, Trillian and Ford explore the underground remains of Magrathean civilisation, leaving Arthur and Marvin on the planet's surface. Arthur bumps into a Magrathean named Slartibartfast who takes him into the planet and shows him the Earth Mk 2 ...

Fit the Fourth:
First broadcast: 29 March 1978

Cast: Peter Jones, Simon Jones, Geoffrey McGivern, Susan Sheridan, Mark Wing-Davey, Richard Vernon, Jim Broadbent, Jonathan Adams, Ray Hassett, Jeremy Browne, Peter Hawkins, David Tate

Story: Slartibartfast explains to Arthur that the Earth was originally built by Magrathea as a commission for the pan-dimensional beings known as mice. Arthur watches recordings that show how the pan-dimensional beings originally built an enormous computer, Deep Thought, to calculate the answer to the great question of life, the universe and everything, which turned out to be 42. A bigger computer, the Earth, was built to find out what the actual question was, but five minutes before the final read-out, the Vogons blew it up.

Arthur meets up with Ford, Zaphod and Trillian who are being entertained by Trillian's white mice. The mice hope that Arthur can help them find the question, but the meeting is interrupted when sirens announce the arrival of galactic cops, chasing the stolen *Heart of Gold*. The four fugitives hide behind a computer bank which then explodes.

Fit the Fifth:
First broadcast: 5 April 1978

Cast: Peter Jones, Simon Jones, Geoffrey McGivern, Susan Sheridan, Mark Wing-Davey, Stephen Moore, Anthony Sharp, Roy Hudd

Story: Recovering from the effects of the exploding computer, Arthur, Ford, Zaphod and Trillian find themselves in Milliways, 'The Restaurant at the End of the Universe'. This is a swish eatery built on the ruins of Magrathea at a point in the space-time continuum just before the heat-death of the universe. They find that Marvin has been on the planet all this time and now works as a Milliways' car park attendant.

Zaphod and Ford take a liking to an extremely black spaceship in the car park and steal it with Marvin's help. However, the ship is outside their control and dumps them into the middle of an intergalactic war.

Fit the Sixth:
First broadcast: 12 April 1978

Cast: Peter Jones, Simon Jones, Geoffrey McGivern, Susan Sheridan, Mark Wing-Davey, Stephen Moore, Aubrey Woods, Jonathan Cecil, David Jason, Beth Porter

Story: Arthur and his friends are dismayed to realise that they have stolen a Haggunenon Admiral's flagship. Haggunenons are super-evolutionary life-forms who constantly change shape – and the Admiral turns out to be the chair they have been sitting in! He evolves into a copy of the Ravenous Bugblatter Beast of Traal and eats Zaphod, Trillian and Marvin, but Ford and Arthur escape in an emergency escape capsule.

The capsule dumps them inside a massive 'ark in space' containing the useless third of the population of the planet Golgafrincham. Commanded by a Captain in a bath, this non-steerable spaceship crash-lands on a primitive planet which they name Fintlewoodlewix but which Ford and Arthur recognise as prehistoric Earth. The arrival of the Golgafrinchans has, unknown to anyone, completely upset the Earth's programming – so it will never produce the right question even if the Vogons don't blow it up. Resigned to their fate, Arthur and Ford wander off to explore the planet.

Background: In February 1977, writer Douglas Adams met with producer Simon Brett to discuss a science fiction comedy series called *The Ends of the Earth*. It was to be an anthology show, in which the world was destroyed in a different way each week. In the first episode, the world was destroyed to make way for a hyper-space bypass. Somehow, that story mutated into *The Hitchhiker's Guide to the Galaxy*.

A pilot script was commissioned in March, written in April and recorded in June.

It wasn't, of course, that simple. Cambridge graduate

Adams had grown up in an era of overblown rock concept albums and wanted his radio series to have similar production values. Not just isolated sound effects but ridiculously huge soundscapes, integrating dialogue, music and wildly imaginative sounds into a holistic presentation. He also wanted a narrator, but not a studio audience. The BBC were adamant that radio comedy had to have an audience or the listeners would not know when to laugh. Simon Brett successfully lobbied for *Hitchhiker's Guide* to be an exception. As for the narrator: every book on radio writing will tell you to avoid this device. It never works. Except (point out the more recent volumes) in the case of *The Hitchhiker's Guide to the Galaxy*. What Adams did was to cleverly integrate his narrator into the story as the audio readout of his intergalactic travel book.

At this point, Adams was 25 and had been scraping a living since graduation with a succession of bizarre jobs while trying to make a go of it as a script writer, but even collaboration with Monty Python's Graham Chapman had not brought him success, and he had only a handful of minor radio and TV credits to his name. All this was about to change.

The first task was to cast the series, and for this Adams turned to his old friends from the Cambridge Footlights Society. The characters of Arthur, Ford and Zaphod were based to some extent on actors Simon Jones, Geoffrey McGivern and Mark Wing-Davey, and the BBC was still sufficiently an old boy network for this casting to be passed.

The biggest problem was the narrator. Adams wanted a 'Peter Jones'-y type of voice, a crisp, English, rather old-world, slightly confused but terribly certain sort of voice. After asking Michael Palin and one or two other people, it was suggested that possibly Peter Jones had a suitably 'Peter Jones'-y voice, and the actor was approached.

The pilot show was recorded in June 1977, with the actors gazing out over the unusually empty stalls of the Paris Studio, London. Two months later, the go-ahead for five more episodes was given. However, by this point Simon Brett was working in television, so the producer's chair was handed over to Geoffrey Perkins (later BBC Head of Comedy).

At this point, the storyline proper began to take shape, although as Perkins recalled: 'Douglas was writing it episode by episode, without any clear idea where he was going, but it meant that if something was good, we could bring it back. Marvin, for example, I said we should keep, but Douglas thought he had used up the idea. I said, "No, look. The whole world of this series keeps changing all the time. We've got to keep some core characters."'

Episodes Two to Four were recorded in November and December 1977, but the final two parts were postponed until February 1978, perilously close to the broadcast date. This was because, after years of relative failure, Adams suddenly found himself writing not only *Hitchhiker's Guide* but *Doctor Who* too. Television schedules being far more immutable than radio ones, *The Pirate Planet* took precedence over *Hitchhiker's Guide*, and when that script was complete, Adams was simply too exhausted to finish the remaining two *Hitchhiker's* episodes.

Enter John Lloyd, a man who subsequently proved to be one of the most important names in British television comedy, helping to create *Not the Nine O'Clock News*, *Spitting Image*, *Blackadder* and the TV version of *Hitchhiker's Guide*. In 1978 he was working for BBC Radio as the producer of *Week Ending*.

Lloyd had known Adams since university and was working on his own science fiction novel, *GiGax*. With Adams needing good, funny, science fiction ideas quick, Lloyd agreed to collaborate on the remaining episodes of *Hitchhiker's*, plundering ideas from his *GiGax* notes. Among his contributions were The Book's speech on the Triganic Pu and other intergalactic currency, and the Haggunenons with their super-evolutionary skills.

The final episode of the first series of *Hitchhiker's* was recorded just eight days before 'Fit the First' was scheduled for broadcast, setting a dangerous precedent in terms of deadlines. The series was favourably reviewed in two Sunday newspapers and, by the end of its first run, had attracted a significant audience, although the BBC remained unsure of what to do with the show. According to Geoffrey Perkins, 'Half way through the first run we got an audience figure in and it was 0.0, which meant that theoretically, no one was listening to it. But I was getting 20–30 letters a day, maybe more.'

Enquiring about further exploitation of the series, Douglas Adams received a letter from BBC Enterprises which said, 'In our experience, books and records of radio series don't sell,' a bad move which may reasonably be compared with Decca turning down the Beatles or Universal passing on the chance to make *Star Wars*. Instead, the novelisation rights went to Pan Books and the album rights to Original Records.

Comment: Although 'Fit the First' offered few clues about where *The Hitchhiker's Guide to the Galaxy* would go – over the next five weeks or the following 27 years – it nevertheless stood out among contemporary radio comedy as something special.

However, in retrospect, the script seems a little formulaic and its Footlights roots show, nowhere more clearly than in the character of Lady Cynthia Fitzmelton. This 'Penelope Keith/Margaret Thatcher type' (played by Jo Kendall of *I'm Sorry I'll Read That Again* and *The Burkiss Way*) has a self-contained monologue in which she officially 'launches' the demolition of Arthur Dent's house, making a small speech before breaking a bottle of champagne on a bulldozer. Dropped from all subsequent versions, Lady Cynthia could have appeared in any Footlights smoking concert of the 1970s without seeming out of place.

There are many other unique aspects to this version which sound odd to those more familiar with the subsequent books and TV series. For example, it seems odd that Arthur, not Ford, persuades Mr Prosser to lie down in the mud. (As Geoffrey Perkins once commented: 'Douglas always had a problem about "What is a character?" – he tended to swap dialogue between characters at will.') But it is in Episodes Five and Six that the radio series shows its uniqueness with the Haggunenon storyline. In all subsequent versions (except a few stage productions), the ship which the main characters steal belongs to the rock group Disaster Area and the Haggunenons have been largely forgotten.

Nevertheless, more than a quarter of a century later, the original six-episode radio series of *Hitchhiker's Guide* remains an extremely funny, and absolutely ground-breaking slice of British radio comedy, as well as a defining moment in the development of science fiction humour.

The Secondary Phase

Fit the Seventh:
First broadcast: 24 December 1978

Cast: Peter Jones, Simon Jones, Geoffrey McGivern, Mark Wing-Davey, Stephen Moore, Bill Paterson, David Tate, Alan Ford

Story: An Arcturan Megafreighter approaching Ursa Minor Beta, home of the *Hitchhiker's Guide to the Galaxy* offices, finds it has an unusual stowaway: Zaphod Beeblebrox. Zaphod escaped from the Haggunenon when it evolved into an escape pod, and then received a message implanted in his brain (by himself) telling him to find a man called Zarniwoop.

Meanwhile, Arthur and Ford are stuck on prehistoric Fintlewoodlewix and are happily drunk when they spot a spaceship fading in and out of reality.

In the lobby of the *Hitchhiker's Guide* offices, Zaphod bumps into Marvin and the two of them head up in the lift to Zarniwoop's office. But the building is attacked by Frogstar fighters looking for Zaphod. Marvin tricks a giant Frogstar robot into destroying itself while Zaphod makes his escape with a strange man named Roosta. But the Frogstar fighters simply steal the whole building, with Zaphod and Roosta inside.

Fit the Eighth:
First broadcast: 21 January 1980

Cast: Peter Jones, Simon Jones, Geoffrey McGivern, Mark Wing-Davey, Stephen Moore, David Tate, Alan Ford, Valentine Dyall

Story: Zaphod and Roosta are taken to the Frogstar, home of the ultimate psychic torture device, the Total Perspective Vortex, and its guardian, Gargravarr. Meanwhile, Ford and Arthur realise that the spaceship they can see will only solidify in their reality if they stop drinking. They do so and the spaceship – the *Heart of Gold* – lands, very heavily and badly. From it staggers Zaphod.

It seems that Ford had somehow lost his towel, which became fossilised, then encased in a meteor derived from the explosion of the Earth. Zaphod found the meteor, spotted the towel and came back in time to rescue them.

Zaphod explains how he escaped from the Total Perspective Vortex. The device is designed to make the victim see how totally insignificant they are in universal terms; Zaphod survived the experience because it showed him that he actually was the most important being in the universe, as he suspected.

Fit the Ninth:
First broadcast: 22 January 1980

Cast: Peter Jones, Simon Jones, Geoffrey McGivern, Mark Wing-Davey, Stephen Moore, Bill Wallis, David Tate, Leueen Willoughby, Richard Goolden

Story: The *Heart of Gold* is pursued by a Vogon fleet, commanded by Prostetnic Vogon Jeltz who is apparently in league with Zaphod's personal analyst, Gag Halfrunt. Arthur finds a Nutrimatic Drinks Dispenser on board and tries to explain to it how to make a cup of tea.

When the Vogons attack, the *Heart of Gold* cannot escape because all its computer circuits have been diverted to Arthur's tea request. Zaphod holds a seance to contact his great grandfather, who is aware of the mission to find Zarniwoop and helpfully solves the problem, thus allowing the ship to escape.

Fit the Tenth:
First broadcast: 23 January 1980

Cast: Peter Jones, Simon Jones, Geoffrey McGivern, Mark Wing-Davey, Stephen Moore, David Tate, Rula Lenska, Ronald Baddiley, John Baddeley, John le Mesurier

Story: The *Heart of Gold* materialises in a strange, smooth cave, high up on the planet Brontitall. Arthur and Marvin fall out of the cave, and Zaphod and Ford nearly follow them.

Arthur lands on the back of a giant bird who shows him that the 'cave' is in fact part of a fifteen-mile-high statue called *Arthur Dent Throwing the Nutrimatic Cup*. Arthur is taken to a bird colony in the statue's ear where he learns how the planet Brontitall became infested with friendly robots. Then one night a vision appeared of Arthur arguing with the Nutrimatic Drinks Dispenser and the people of Brontitall realised that they did not have to be friendly back to the robots, so they banished them from the planet and built the statue in Arthur's honour. They later evolved into birds because of a second plague which they are reluctant to discuss.

Ford and Zaphod fall out of the cup, also landing on a bird. Meanwhile Arthur travels down to the planet's surface, where he is attacked by a foot warrior from the Dolmansaxlil Shoe Corporation but rescued by an attractive archaeologist named Lintilla.

Fit the Eleventh:
First broadcast: 24 January 1980

Cast: Peter Jones, Simon Jones, Geoffrey McGivern, Mark Wing-Davey, Stephen Moore, David Tate, Rula Lenska, John Baddeley, Mark Smith

Story: As Ford and Zaphod escape from a flock of angry birds, Lintilla introduces Arthur to Lintilla and Lintilla, explaining that due to an accident there are 578,000,000,000 Lintilla clones in the universe. The other Lintillas are delighted that their archaeological dig has suddenly been helped by the unexplained opening up of a deep shaft (caused, unknown to them, by Marvin's plummet from the cup).

A layer of crushed shoes explains the planet's second plague. It passed the Shoe Event Horizon, the point at which only shoe shops are built and the economy collapses. Arthur and the Lintillas are captured by a Dolmansaxlil executive who shows them why shoes are important, but they are rescued by Marvin.

Meanwhile, Ford and Arthur escape the birds by hiding in a derelict spaceport where, incredibly, one spaceship seems to be still functioning.

Fit the Twelfth:
First broadcast: 25 January 1980

Cast: Peter Jones, Simon Jones, Geoffrey McGivern, Mark Wing-Davey, Stephen Moore, David Tate, Rula Lenska, Ken Campbell, Jonathan Pryce

Story: Escaping from the Dolmansaxlil headquarters, Arthur, Marvin and the three Lintillas encounter a man named Poodoo, who is accompanied by a priest and three male anticlones all called Allitnil. The Lintillas and Allitnils instantly fall in love and Poodoo's priest sets about marrying them, whereupon they disappear.

As Zaphod and Ford explore the spaceship, the passengers all suddenly wake up and start panicking. Zaphod and Ford seek refuge in the cockpit where they meet ... Zarniwoop!

With one Allitnil dead, Arthur, Marvin and the remaining Lintilla make their escape to the abandoned spaceport. Zarniwoop explains to Ford and Zaphod that they have been in an artificial universe all along. It was all a plan to bring Zarniwoop the *Heart of Gold*, the only ship capable of taking him to the home of the ruler of the universe.

On an otherwise uninhabited planet, a man lives in a shack with his pet cat. Zarniwoop, Zaphod, Arthur and Ford visit him – for he is the ruler of the universe. The reason that he is capable of ruling is that he believes only what he can see and hear himself, so he does not believe that the rest of the universe exists and can therefore make completely objective decisions.

The man lets slip that Zaphod was behind the analysts' and Vogons' plan to destroy the Earth, and Arthur, in a huff, returns to the *Heart of Gold*. As the ship blasts off with Arthur, Lintilla and Marvin on board, Zaphod, Ford and Zarniwoop are left stranded on the planet ...

Background: Although generally considered part of series two (or '*The Secondary Phase*' as it became known much later), 'Fit the Seventh' was written and recorded entirely separately. It was recorded in November 1978 and broadcast over Christmas, more than a year before 'Fit the Eighth'. To all intents and purposes, this was *The Hitchhiker's Guide to the Galaxy Christmas Special* – however, as Douglas Adams subsequently pointed out: 'It had nothing to do with Christmas and was not aired on Christmas Day. Those are the only two known connections with Christmas.'

The original plan had been to base the story around the Nativity, with the star that guides the Wise Men actually being the hapless Marvin plummeting through the atmosphere and smashing into a Bethlehem stable. Given the controversy which surrounded the release of *Monty Python's Life of Brian* the following year, the decision to abandon this storyline was remarkably prudent. By this point, the first series had already been repeated twice, and Douglas Adams was busy writing the novelisation.

The second series hit problems almost straight away. 'Fit

the Eighth' took three days to record in May 1979, and 'Fit the Ninth' was postponed the following month. Part of the problem was that Adams was still desperately trying to finish his novel.

In May, *Hitchhiker's Guide* was adapted as a stage play; in July it was re-recorded as an LP; in August it was nominated for an award at the World Science Fiction Convention. 'Fit the Ninth' was finally committed to tape in November; 'Fit the Tenth' followed in December, by which time Adams was already working on a pilot script for a TV version. The final two episodes were recorded in January, just in time for broadcast. 'Fit the Twelfth' was in fact still being mixed less than an hour before it was due to air, and was subsequently remixed for repeats.

The five shows were broadcast in a single week and featured on the cover of *Radio Times*. However, as the magazine went to press before the final episode was recorded, the character of the Man in the Shack was still uncast and was credited to the anagrammatic Ron Hate (it was actually Stephen Moore).

Comment: The second radio series is one of the forgotten gems of the *Hitchhiker's* canon. Although a few of the ideas were raised briefly in the second novel, knowledge of this storyline is evidence of a real *Hitchhiker's Guide* fan.

There are some fantastic ideas here, possibly too many: the Total Perspective Vortex, the Shoe Event Horizon, the plague of robots, the statue of Arthur Dent (with its giant floating cup held in position by art), the Lintilla clones and the ruler of the Universe.

Because of the limits of the six-part series (or strictly speaking, a special and a five-part series), and especially because of the desperate rush to record the final three episodes, much of the script seems rushed and no sooner are we introduced to one plot point than we have to move on to another. Nevertheless, true fans of *Hitchhiker's Guide* rate the second radio series very highly.

In 1985, all 12 radio scripts were published as *The Hitchhiker's Guide to the Galaxy: The Original Radio Scripts*, including copious amounts of unheard material and extensive footnotes by both Douglas Adams and Geoffrey Perkins.

Sheila's Ear

Also known as 'Fit the Six-and-a-halfth', this mini-episode was broadcast on 4 August 1982 as part of a one-off show called *Steafel Plus*, starring comedienne Sheila Steafel. Arthur was surprised to find himself being interviewed on Radio 4, but soon discovered that he was merely dreaming and was still stuck on prehistoric Earth; this revelation neatly slotted 'Sheila's Ear' into the *Hitchhiker's Guide* canon between the sixth and seventh episodes.

Because this sketch was never documented, its existence remained unknown for 20 years – although a few off-air recordings existed in private hands. It was rediscovered in 2002; the script was included in a '25th Anniversary Edition' of the radio scripts in 2003; and in 2004 this 'lost episode' was included on the CD set *Douglas Adams at the BBC*.

The Tertiary Phase

First broadcast: 21 September – 24 October 2004

Cast: William Franklyn, Simon Jones, Geoffrey McGivern, Susan Sheridan, Mark Wing-Davey, Stephen Moore, Roger Gregg, Richard Griffiths, Leslie Philips, Joanna Lumley, Chris Langham, Douglas Adams

Story: *The Tertiary Phase* is a reasonably faithful adaptation of *Life, the Universe and Everything*. However, as this book starts from the end of the first radio series, with Arthur and Ford on prehistoric Earth, the entire second series had to be explained away as a psychotic episode which only Zaphod experienced.

Background: BBC Enterprises came up with the idea of a third radio series of *Hitchhiker's Guide* in 1993 when they noticed how well the tapes and CDs of the original series were selling.

After Neil Gaiman turned down the job, a writer named Alick Rowe was set the task of adapting *Life, the Universe and Everything* into an eight-part radio series. Producer Dirk Maggs was appointed to oversee the project, scheduled to be recorded in October that year and broadcast in November. The original cast were contacted, and Brian Johnstone and Fred Trueman agreed to play the cricket commentators in the first episode.

Unfortunately, Rowe's first draft was deemed unsuitable. Douglas Adams wrote a first episode to show how the adaptation should be done, but did not have time to write the rest of the series, and the project was 'put on hold' before fading away. A brief attempt to revive it in 1997 was stymied by developments with the movie, the contract for which included other media rights.

In 2002, after Adams' death, an independent radio producer, Bryce Hyman, became involved for the first time. The rights were acquired by Hyman's production company, Above the Title, with Dirk Maggs as adapter, director and co-producer. The surviving original cast were reunited and the six episodes were recorded in November 2003 for broadcast on BBC Radio 4 in February and March 2004. However, there were still legal problems regarding the movie, which was by then in pre-production, and broadcast was delayed until September. The episodes were also made available over the Internet in Dolby 5.1 surround sound.

Douglas Adams had told Maggs that he hoped to play Agrajag himself and this was achieved posthumously by editing in that character's dialogue from the Adams-read unabridged audiobook of *Life, the Universe and Everything*.

Comment: Radio is the natural home of *The Hitchhiker's Guide to the Galaxy* and many people were understandably delighted to hear new radio episodes, nearly a quarter of a century after the last series. As before, the series was at the cutting edge of radio technology: Maggs' production was superb, perfectly in tune with Douglas Adams' original intention that the show should sound 'like a rock album'. Dialogue, sound effects, background voices and original music by Adams' friend Paul 'Wix' Wickens were woven into a multi-layered whole.

The cast slipped back into character with consummate ease, with William Franklyn ably replacing his friend Peter Jones and a nice gag in the first episode to explain the *Guide*'s new voice. Among the new cast, Andy Taylor's role as Zem the Mattress was hilarious and an indisputable highlight of the series.

The problem, if there was one, lay in the scripts and was really unavoidable. Maggs put a great deal of work into the adaptation (his proposed co-writer having been vetoed by the Adams estate for unclear reasons). Adams' own script was split over the first two episodes in order to introduce Zaphod, Trillian and Marvin in 'Fit the Thirteenth' rather than concentrating exclusively on Arthur and Ford. But a degree of reverence to the original material was essential to please the fans, so Maggs did not have the liberty to make suggestions for improvements that Geoffrey Perkins had enjoyed in 1978. This took away the freewheeling, anything-can-happen nature of *Hitchhiker's Guide*. On the positive side, *Life, the Universe and Everything* at least has a coherent plot (even if it is reliant on *deus ex machina* events) because of its origins as a *Doctor Who* story.

The Quandary and Quintessential Phases
Broadcast: 3 May – 21 June 2005

Cast: William Franklyn, Simon Jones, Susan Sheridan, Geoffrey McGivern, Stephen Moore, Mark Wing-Davey, Stephen Fry, Christian Slater, Saeed Jaffrey, Miriam Margolyes, Chris Emmett, Michael Cule, Jackie Mason, Jonathan Pryce, Rula Lenska, David Dixon, Sandra Dickinson, June Whitfield, Arthur Smith, Bill Paterson,

Geoffrey Perkins, Griff Rhys Jones, Andrew Secombe, Roy Hudd, Douglas Adams

Not broadcast when this new edition was written, these two back-to-back four-part adaptations of *So Long ...* and *Mostly Harmless* completed the saga of *Hitchhiker's Guide* on radio. The scripts were once again by Dirk Maggs, but whereas *The Tertiary Phase* had stuck rigidly to its source, series four and five introduced some new ideas and played with some established storylines, creating a continuous saga which incorporated not only the contradictory *Secondary Phase* but also the TV series.

The Vogons, absent from the fourth book but reintroduced in the fifth, made an appearance in *The Quandary Phase* for continuity's sake, while Zaphod and Zarniwoop were included in *The Quintessential Phase* in a scene which linked back to the Total Perspective Vortex.

Maggs' development of the theme of multiple universes, introduced by Douglas Adams in the fifth book, allowed the incorporation of cast members from other versions. Since there are two versions of Trillian in the last book, Maggs cleverly cast both Sheridan and Dickinson, while Rula Lenska (Lintilla in *The Secondary Phase*) provided the voice of the new, birdlike edition of the *Guide* itself.

Douglas Adams had often expressed dissatisfaction with the ending of *Mostly Harmless*, written under enormous stress to hit a much-delayed deadline. So, although Maggs knew that Adams had wanted a faithful *Tertiary Phase*, with Series Four and especially Series Five he strove to be true to the spirit of the series rather than the letter of the books, including two alternative endings to the very final episode.

Once again, extended versions of the episodes were made available on CD.

3. The Stage Productions

It may surprise many people to discover that the first ever adaptation of *The Hitchhiker's Guide to the Galaxy* – before it was a book, a TV series, an LP or even a second radio series – was a stage play. For more than 20 years, *Hitchhiker's Guide* has been a popular, if intermittent, title in the theatrical world. It has been performed on three continents, by a wide variety of professional and amateur casts. However, it is the first three productions which are of most note.

The Science Fiction Theatre of Liverpool Production

Dates: May 1979
Venue: Institute for Contemporary Arts, London
Director: Ken Campbell

Cast: Chris Langham, Richard Hope, Mitch Davies, Stephen Williams, Sue Jones-Davies, Russell Denton, Cindy Oswin, Maya Sendalle, Roger Sloman, John Joyce, Neil Cunningham

Ken Campbell is a legend of British theatre, and his

Science Fiction Theatre of Liverpool was responsible for such memorable productions as *Illuminatus!*, *The Warp* (the longest play ever performed), and *The Hitchhiker's Guide to the Galaxy*, which he adapted himself from the first series' radio scripts.

Realising that an offbeat, original story like *Hitchhiker's Guide* required an offbeat, original presentation, Campbell hit on the inspired notion of reversing the traditional physical structure of a theatre. Rather than have the audience sit passively while the actors strode on and off stage, he devised a way for the actors to remain stationary while the audience moved around.

To this end, a seating platform was built which worked on a hovercraft principle. Balancing on a cushion of air a fraction of a millimetre above the floor of the ICA auditorium, it could be pushed around by stage hands, thus pointing the audience towards whichever of the actors (scattered around the walls on platforms of various heights) was talking.

Of course, this technique severely limited the size of the audience, with only 80 seats available for each of the nine performances. The show sold out in a flash and there was simply no way that any extra seats could be found – even for the radio cast. As Simon Jones recalled: 'When I said I was Arthur Dent they looked at me as though I'd said I was the Queen of Sheba.'

The problem of Zaphod's second head was solved by having two actors strapped together in one costume, while The Book's narration was, in a never-repeated touch, shared between two usherettes, named Lithos and Terros. Cindy Oswin, who played Lithos, shortly afterwards played Trillian on the *Hitchhiker's Guide* LPs. Campbell himself would play Poodoo in the final episode of the second radio series.

Arthur was played by Chris Langham who was only available because the first series of *Not the Nine O'Clock News*, in which he was a regular, had been postponed until after the general election. Twenty-five years later he returned to *Hitchhiker's Guide* as Prak in *The Tertiary Phase*.

In direct contrast to the success of the small-scale ICA production, the second (and last) London production of *Hitchhiker's Guide* would prove to be an unmitigated disaster.

The Rainbow Theatre Production

Dates: July–August 1980
Venue: Rainbow Theatre, London
Director: Ken Campbell

Cast: Roger Blake, Kim Durham, David Brett, John Terence, Nicholas d'Avirro, Jude Alderson, David Learner, Mike Cule, Lewis Cowen, James Castle, David Atkinson, Beverly Andrews, Doretta Dunkley, Kenteas Brine

Though it has been a success in many media in many countries, *Hitchhiker's Guide* is not invulnerable and the West End production remains a classic example of how it can be done wrong. Where the ICA production had been low-key fringe theatre, cleverly making a virtue out of its scanty budget and minimal special effects, the Rainbow production was a huge, overblown rock opera.

The Rainbow, long since closed (in fact the failure of this show contributed to its demise) was a 1930s building which, in the late 1970s, had become more of a rock venue than a theatre. This, combined with the presence of a live rock group providing incidental music, led some reviewers to inaccurately label the production as a musical.

Mike Cule – who at various times played Prostetnic Vogon Jeltz, Deep Thought, Hotblack Desiato's body-guard, the Dish of the Day, the Captain of the 'B' Ark and the voice of a mouse – remembered the opening night with horror: 'Backstage was a little chaotic. They were still making my Vogon costume when I put it on, and the second half hadn't had a technical rehearsal.' It didn't help that the actors playing Ford and Arthur had swapped roles with each other only a week before.

Two thousand *Hitchhiker's* fans – almost three times as many as had seen the entire run of the ICA production – were treated to a show which could most charitably be described as long. Adapted, like the ICA version, from the radio scripts, the Rainbow production had kept in all those elements which the previous play had deleted or minimised. Consequently, the show was more than three hours long, a problem exacerbated by the band's insistence on performing an entire 35-minute set during the Milliways' scene. By the time the curtain fell, well after midnight, all but the hardiest of the audience had long since departed.

'I saw the productions at the ICA, Clwyd and the Rainbow,' said radio producer Geoffrey Perkins. 'The ICA had the incredible hovercraft which to a certain extent covered up the details of the show which were a little rough. The Rainbow production of course was a disaster, which lost all the detail of Douglas' writing.'

The critics tore the show to shreds and, although drastic measures were taken to cut the script and tighten up the production, the audience rapidly dwindled away to almost nothing. When the show finally closed, five weeks into its projected eight-week run, it was regularly playing to audiences of 50 or 60 – ironically smaller than those who had sat on the ICA's hovercraft. The producers disappeared, owing cast, crew and venue considerable amounts of money. Nobody would ever be crazy enough to stage *Hitchhiker's Guide* as a spectacular again. From now on, productions would stick to enthusiasm and a lot of imagination, best exemplified by the now standard technique of representing the council bulldozer with a Tonka toy.

Aside from the terrible reviews and chaotic opening night, the Rainbow production was memorable for two innovations. It was one of the first ever West End shows to incorporate lasers, much to the concern of the GLC Health and Safety Department. It also saw the first ever appearance of the Dish of the Day, the ruminant specially bred to want to be eaten. Two of the cast went on to appear in the TV series: Mike Cule as the Vogon Guard in Episode Two and David Learner inside the Marvin costume.

In-between these two extremes, came the first provincial production of *Hitchhiker's Guide*, and the only stage version ever to tour.

The Theatr Clwyd Productions

Dates: January–February 1980
Venues: Theatres in Bangor, Aberystwyth, Cardiff and Mold
Director: Jonathan Petherbridge
Cast included: Roger Blake, Mike Burns, David Learner

Like the Rainbow production, the Theatr Clwyd version was adapted fairly literally from the radio scripts, this time by Jonathan Petherbridge. Unlike the West End disaster, however, this version was produced by people who knew how reluctant most people would be to sit through a three-hour sci-fi comedy.

Petherbridge's solution was to stage two episodes each night on Tuesday, Wednesday and Thursday, then perform the whole six-part play for the hardcore fans on Friday and Saturday.

The most memorable element of the Theatr Clwyd production by far was the Haggunenon. While the subsequent TV series would shy away from showing a pilot's chair mutating into a carbon copy of the Ravenous Bugblatter Beast of Traal, Petherbridge felt that this was precisely the sort of effect which could not only be achieved on the stage of a small Welsh theatre, but could then be packed away and easily transported to other small Welsh theatres.

The result was a huge inflatable Haggunenon – once seen, never forgotten – which was later loaned out to other stage productions preferring to follow the original storyline.

Greeted with both critical and popular acclaim,

Petherbridge later shorted his script into a manageable two-act play, which subsequently became the standard stage version, although it was never actually published. The Theatr Clwyd 'Special Edition' toured England and Wales in late 1981. Starting at Theatr Clwyd's base in Mold in October, it travelled to Cambridge, Newcastle-upon-Tyne, Cardiff, Bristol, Stirling, Poole, Warwick and Swansea before finishing its run in December at Oxford Playhouse.

From the original production Roger Blake and David Learner reprised their roles as The Book and Marvin, having suffered the Rainbow fiasco in the interim. Also in the cast were Jon Strickland, Mike Burns, Harriet Keevil, Lewis Cowen, Andy Whitfield, Leader Hawkins, Tony Welch, Lizzi Cocker and Ken Ellis. Ellis, a professional puppeteer, was an unusual Zaphod in that his second head spent much of its time held in his right hand.

More Professional Productions

Hitchhiker's Guide next appeared in the Drum studio at the Theatre Royal, Plymouth (May–June 1982), again directed by Jonathan Petherbridge, and with David Learner making his fourth and last stage appearance as Marvin. Linda Dobell was the first actress to play The Book (the ICA's twin usherettes notwithstanding), a casting decision which later became something of a tradition, largely because there is only one other female role in the play. Still innovating, Petherbridge staged the Milliways scene in the Theatre Royal's bar, but after complaints from patrons attending the main theatre's production of *Jesus Christ Superstar*, the scene was moved back into the studio.

Derby Playhouse was the next venue to stage the Petherbridge adaptation (September–October 1982), this time directed by Christopher Honer. The show was next presented at the Belgrade Theatre, Coventry (June–July 1983) in a production of the Petherbridge script directed by Rob Bettinson. Lewis Cowen, who had played small roles for the Rainbow and Theatre Clwyd, finally came to the fore as The Book.

Finally, the one and only overseas professional production was staged at the La Boite Theatre in Brisbane, Australia from October to December 1983, proving so popular that its run was extended by a week. The script by Daniel Murphy was an original adaptation, taking in elements of both the Rainbow script and the Petherbridge adaptation. For simplicity's sake, Zaphod was given only one head and two arms.

Unfortunately, by this time plans were well under way for the feature film version, and as is common with film rights, the picture's 'in development' status precluded any professional stage productions. However, that clause in the film contract has not hampered the amateur dramatic scene.

Amateur Productions

It is believed that the first ever amateur stage production of *Hitchhiker's Guide* was actually American, performed by students at a school in Hanover, New Hampshire some time in the autumn of 1982. Lacking access to the Petherbridge version or the radio scripts, the play was adapted directly from the novel.

The Theatr Clwyd inflatable Haggunenon reappeared

in a production at the Crescent Theatre, Birmingham in February and March 1985, the same year that *Hitchhiker's Guide* was performed by students at Haywards Heath College, Hampshire. A version performed by RATS (Redditch Amateur Theatrical Society) at the Palace Theatre, Reditch in November 1986 also used the Haggunenon storyline, but kept the creature itself off-stage. This production was also notable for a Marvin costume which was a large, silver-covered cardboard box, and for featuring the only ever stage appearance of Lady Cynthia Fitzmelton, the civic dignitary who broke champagne on the bulldozers before they demolished Arthur's house in the first radio episode.

One of the most bizarre stage productions was that performed at the Comedia Colonia in Germany in February 1987, which was a one-man show. Axel Pape was the one man, and by all accounts the play was very entertaining. Two months later, a production at the Portsmouth Drama Centre, Southsea established its own unique place in the field by incorporating scenes from the third and fourth novels, as well as a cameo appearance by Eccentrica Gallumbits, the triple-breasted whore of Eroticon VI (a character who, though mentioned, has never actually appeared in any other version of *Hitchhiker's Guide*).

The next production was at the Loft Theatre, Leamington Spa in December 1988, while 1990 saw two amdram versions: one by the Romsey Operatic and Dramatic Society, and one by the Menlo Players Guild of California, who enjoyed the experience so much that they staged the play again in 1994.

In May 1992, the Jonathan Petherbridge adaptation

resurfaced in, of all places, Bermuda. Most impressively, the audience on the opening night of the Bermuda Musical and Dramatic Society's production included Prince Edward, who was touring the Caribbean at the time.

Always popular with students, *Hitchhiker's Guide* was performed at Liverpool John Moore's University in December 1994 and at Barry Boys' School, South Wales in March 1995. In June 1996, children at Wildern School, Southampton, who had been studying the novel in English lessons, produced their own dramatised version from scratch in less than a week as an end of term project.

The Strathclyde Theatre Company in October 1996 performed an adaptation of the radio scripts on stage as a radio play, standing around microphones and even wearing BBC-style evening dress. The play was presented in Linz, Austria in 1998 and a half-hour extract was performed at the University of Hawaii in April 1999. A group of German students staged *Hitchhiker's Guide* at Brechtbau in February 2000 and again at Freiberg in May of that year. New York's Reverie Productions performed the radio scripts of the first six episodes, with sound effects, on stage in February 2002 and a similar production was staged in Naples, Florida in February 2004, while a more conventional version turned up at the Spaganga Theatre, San Francisco in December 2003.

Possibly the oddest version of all was that performed by the Arena Theatre Company at the Regent Centre, Christchurch, Dorset in May 1995. This was the much threatened 'musical version' with the cast breaking into a variety of 1960s pop songs, such as *Don't They Know It's the End of the World?* The result, apparently, was dire.

4. The Books

The Hitchhiker's Guide to the Galaxy

Paperback: Pan Books, October 1979
Hardback: Arthur Barker Ltd, February 1980

Story: Arthur Dent wakes up, finds that his house is about to be knocked down, learns that his friend Ford Prefect is an alien and is rescued when the Vogons destroy Earth. Far away on the planet Damogran, Galactic President Zaphod Beeblebrox steals the fantastic *Heart of Gold* spaceship which he is supposed to be launching.

Ford introduces Arthur to Babel Fish, towels and *The Hitchhiker's Guide to the Galaxy*, but they are captured by the Vogons and thrown into space. Fortunately they are rescued by the *Heart of Gold*, which is crewed by Zaphod, his girlfriend Trillian and Marvin the paranoid android.

Zaphod takes the *Heart of Gold* to Magrathea, dormant home of a fabulously wealthy planet-building industry, and after a close shave involving two guided missiles, the ship lands. Zaphod, Ford and Trillian go exploring, while Arthur meets Slartibartfast and Marvin stays by the ship.

Slartibartfast tells Arthur of the Earth's origins as a giant computer built by pan-dimensional beings to find the question of life, the universe and everything, after the great computer Deep Thought announced that the answer was 42. Trillian's white mice want to dissect Arthur's brain, but he makes his escape along with Ford, Zaphod and Trillian. They are cornered by two galactic cops, who are killed when their life-support systems blow up. Returning to the *Heart of Gold*, they find that Marvin had talked the cops' shipboard computer into killing itself, and hence the cops.

Leaving Magrathea, the *Heart of Gold* and its crew head for the restaurant at the end of the universe …

Background: *The Hitchhiker's Guide to the Galaxy* was written by Douglas Adams in late 1978 and the first half of 1979. By August 1979 (when *Hitchhiker's* was nominated for the World Science Fiction Award or 'Hugo', losing out as Best Dramatic Presentation to *Superman: The Movie*), adverts were starting to appear, but there was no sign of the book.

The original plan had been for the novel to recount the storyline of the radio series, but in the end it only covered episodes one to four, and thus did not include any of John Lloyd's material from 'Fit the Fifth' and 'Fit the Sixth'. (Adams had originally considered co-writing the book with John Lloyd, but subsequently opted to be sole author.) An apocryphal story tells how, as the print deadline loomed, an exasperated Pan executive supposedly told Adams to 'finish the page you're working on' before spiriting away the manuscript, glad to at least have something long enough to publish as a novel.

An initial print run of 60,000 copies was ordered, and

Pan's faith in the project was justified when the book entered the bestseller charts at number nine. Within three months it had sold 250,000 copies. In January 1984, Douglas received a Golden Pan award from his publishers when paperback sales of the book broke one million.

Comment: For many people, the novel of *The Hitchhiker's Guide to the Galaxy* is their introduction to the story as a whole, and in many ways it is the definitive text. Certainly the radio series came first, but with the novel Douglas Adams was able to eliminate some of the less satisfactory parts of the story, and tidy up those which almost, but not quite, worked.

Given the chance to expand and reinvent the story from scratch, Adams goes off on wild flights of fancy into areas unexplored elsewhere in the *Hitchhiker's Guide* canon, such as the actual theft of the *Heart of Gold*. It is worth reflecting that, when he wrote this, he cannot have imagined that 23 years later people would not only still be reading the book, but would still be listening to the radio series on which it was based and comparing the two.

This is one of those novels which can be returned to time and time again, the jokes that seemed so fresh and original on first reading turning into comfortably familiar friends. But there are also many delights to be spotted, especially when returning to the novel after many years, and familiarity with the other versions. The footnote in Chapter Four, for example, which mentions that only six people in the universe know where the real power lies, ties in directly with 'Fit the Twelfth' (Adams wrote the novel and second radio series simultaneously).

The Restaurant at the End of the Universe

Paperback: Pan Books, October 1980
Hardback: Arthur Barker Ltd, February 1981

Story: Prostetnic Vogon Jeltz, in league with Zaphod's analyst Gag Halfrunt, is tracking the *Heart of Gold*. As the Vogons move in to attack, Eddie the computer announces that all his circuits are taken up with Arthur's request for a cup of tea, so Zaphod organises a seance to contact his great grandfather.

The ghost somehow causes the *Heart of Gold* to leap out of danger while simultaneously making Arthur a pot of tea, but in the process Zaphod and Marvin disappear. Zaphod reappears outside the offices of *The Hitchhiker's Guide to the Galaxy*, aware that he has to find a man called Zarniwoop. He bumps into Marvin on the way to Zarniwoop's office, then meets Roosta as the building is attacked by Frogstar fighters. Marvin distracts then destroys a giant robot while Zaphod and Roosta escape but the whole building is torn from its foundations and taken to Frogstar World B.

Zaphod meets Gargravarr, custodian of the Total Perspective Vortex, who explains how the planet's population mutated into birds after passing the Shoe Event Horizon. After surviving the Total Perspective Vortex's torture, because it merely panders to his ego, Zaphod finds a derelict spaceport where one ship still works. When the passengers wake up and panic, Zaphod retreats to the cockpit where he meets ... Zarniwoop.

Zarniwoop switches off his artificial universe and Zaphod discovers that the *Heart of Gold* was actually miniaturised and in his pocket all along. Reunited with Ford, Trillian and Arthur, Zaphod asks Eddie the computer to send them to the nearest place to eat, whereupon the four of them disappear in a puff of smoke.

They come to in Milliways, 'The Restaurant at the End of the Universe', where Ford meets an old friend, rock star Hotblack Desiato, and Arthur is revolted by an animal that wants to be eaten. Marvin telephones them from the car park, having stayed on Frogstar World B for 576,000,000,000 years, and helps them steal an extremely black spaceship.

Unable to control the ship, they discover that it belongs to Hotblack's band, Disaster Area, and is programmed to crash into a star. Marvin operates the emergency teleport, allowing the others to escape. Arthur and Ford materialise on the Golgafrinchan 'B' Ark, which then crashes into a planet. The Golgafrinchans name it Fintlewoodlewix but Arthur and Ford realise that they are on prehistoric Earth, which can now never function as it should. Resigned to their fate, they wander off to explore the planet.

Background: *The Restaurant at the End of the Universe* was a direct sequel to *The Hitchhiker's Guide to the Galaxy*. With the first novel having ended so abruptly, a follow-up was inevitable and, like its predecessor, this book rocketed up the bestseller charts. Ostensibly adapted from episodes five to twelve of the radio series, it is in fact based largely on 'Fit the Fifth' and 'Fit the Sixth', with the Disaster Area storyline replacing John Lloyd's Haggunenon sequence and disparate sequences from *The Secondary Phase* integrated into the plot.

Comment: In many ways, this is the most satisfying of the five *Hitchhiker's Guide* novels. What could have been merely the final chapters of *The Hitchhiker's Guide to the Galaxy* is expanded into a book which takes the reader all over the universe, reinvents ideas from the entirety of the radio series and really fleshes out the characters, both principal and minor.

There is the same lightness of tone as the first book, but with a not unexpected maturity and confidence in the writing. The central Milliways' sequence in particular is a joy to read, including the Dish of the Day scene which had been originally written for the Rainbow Theatre production.

The book finishes in the same place as the TV series and the first radio series, with Arthur and Ford on prehistoric Earth, a 'full circle' structure which brings the story to a completely satisfying conclusion. It is a testament to Adams' growing literary skills that he was able to incorporate into this storyline elements such as Zaphod's visit to the Total Perspective Vortex and the Man in the Shack, which followed afterwards in the radio series.

Restaurant ... is just the right length, just the right depth, and very, very funny. The only reason not to recommend this book as a starting point for those new to *Hitchhiker's Guide* is that, without having read the first book, it won't make sense.

Life, the Universe and Everything

Paperback: Pan Books, August 1982
Hardback: Arthur Barker Ltd, September 1982

Story: After Arthur is insulted by an immortal being named Wowbagger the Infinitely Prolonged, he and Ford are transported to Lord's Cricket Ground where they meet Slartibartfast and witness a squad of deadly, cricket-playing robots steal the ashes. Marvin, who now has an artificial leg, meets a mattress called Zem but is then kidnapped by the cricket-playing robots. Trillian leaves Zaphod on the *Heart of Gold*, which is then attacked by the robots, who shoot Zaphod and steal the Infinite Improbability Drive.

Ford and Arthur learn how the planet Krikkit existed inside a dust cloud so the inhabitants never knew there were any other stars or worlds; when the people of Krikkit finally discovered the galaxy, they decided to destroy it. Eventually defeated, Krikkit was locked in a time-loop, the key to which was based on the galaxy's symbol of prosperity, the wicket. The key was blasted into pieces when a rogue Krikkit warship tried to seize it.

Slartibartfast, Arthur and Ford teleport into a flying party, searching for the silver bail, but Arthur's teleport goes awry and he finds himself confronted by an aggrieved being called Agrajag who has been reincarnated many times, each time being accidentally killed by Arthur. He tries to kill Arthur but dies again after revealing that Arthur will be nearly assassinated on Stavromula Beta.

Arthur falls off a mountain, accidentally learns to fly

and gets hit by the party, where he meets Ford, Slartibartfast, Trillian and a man who won a Rory award. The robots appear and steal the Rory.

After the Krikkit robots release their planet from its time-loop, the quartet descend to the planet where they find a confused population. Zaphod also sneaks down to Krikkit where he discovers that the robots have all become depressed because Marvin is plugged into their central computer.

Trillian correctly deduces that Krikkit has been controlled all along by a megalomaniac computer, Hactar, which once tried to destroy the universe but failed. Hactar was believed destroyed but in fact formed the dust-cloud around Krikkit, which is now dispersed, saving the universe.

Arthur and friends find a man called Prak who explains to them that simultaneous knowledge of the ultimate question and the ultimate answer is logically impossible. He also tells them where to find God's final message to His creation. Later, Arthur meets Wowbagger again.

Background: 'After I wrote the second book I was utterly, completely determined that this was it – there would not be another *Hitchhiker* book,' Douglas Adams told an interviewer, when *Life, the Universe and Everything* was published. 'After the third one, I also say I'm not going to do another one.'

For the first time, Pan promoted the book with extensive point of sale material, including the now infamous 'cans of everything' which were given away to reviewers and a few fortunate fans. This book won Douglas Adams his third Golden Pan when sales passed one million copies. Mini-hardbacks of the first three *Hitchhiker's* novels were published by Millennium in 1994, complete with a facsimile Douglas Adams' signature.

For a brief guide to discrepancies between the British and American editions of *Life, the Universe and Everything*, see Chapter Eight.

Comment: Anybody expecting a novelisation of the second radio series (or rather, the bits of it not in *The Restaurant at the End of the Universe*) was in for a surprise with this book, although this wasn't a completely new story. It was a reworking of an unfilmed *Doctor Who* treatment, *Doctor Who and the Krikkitmen*, which Adams had written long before *Hitchhiker's Guide*.

And frankly, you can tell. It's not that *Life, the Universe and Everything* is a bad book. It's a very good book – well-written and very funny. It's just not a *Hitchhiker's Guide to the Galaxy* book and it sits uneasily in the series, sandwiched in-between the first two novels (young, fresh, exciting, adapted freely from the radio series) and the final two (mature, introspective, original). In particular, Slartibartfast seems out of place, a completely different character to the one in the first novel and the radio and TV series. The original Slartibartfast was a meek ditherer, but this one has been given the Doctor's lines, so he is dynamic and feels it's up to him to save the universe. (Later in the story Slartibartfast fades into the background as Trillian takes over the Doctor's dialogue.)

There are some terrific ideas in *Life, the Universe and Everything*: bistromathics, the flying party, and especially

Agrajag. Agrajag is a superbly inventive way of explaining the first book's bowl of petunias gag, which could have not only fallen flat but spoiled the original joke. However, other characters are not as memorable as they should be, and the whole climactic sequence with Prak fails to provide the sort of satisfying conclusion that the second book managed. Nor do Wowbagger the Infinitely Prolonged's book-ending cameos give the book a satisfying structure, being far too obvious an attempt to create a circular narrative. The storyline as a whole is also slightly unsatisfying as the heroes spend most of the book chasing helplessly after the robots, failing to prevent them from reassembling the key.

Which is a shame because the book is in many other ways very enjoyable. It also has, in its original Pan paperback incarnation, easily the best cover of any *Hitchhiker's Guide* novel.

So Long, and Thanks for All the Fish

Hardback: Pan Books, November 1984
Paperback: Pan Books, November 1985

Story: After eight years of travelling through space and time, Arthur Dent returns home to Earth, and is rather alarmed to discover that he has arrived *after* the date on which he knows the planet was destroyed. He meets a young woman named Fenchurch, who had been sitting in a café in Rickmansworth on the day that the world was 'destroyed' – an event which is now put down to mass hallucination.

Arthur's home is as untidy as he left it, except that somebody has left him a beautifully made goldfish bowl, inscribed with the words, 'So long and thanks.' Besotted by thoughts of Fenchurch, he meets her for a second time and discovers that she has the unusual capacity of walking very slightly above the ground, which prompts him to teach her how to fly.

Arthur learns that on the day when everyone imagined the world being destroyed, all the dolphins disappeared. He also discovers that Fenchurch has a fishbowl just like his. Together they travel to California to meet a man called Wonko the Sane, whose house is built inside out. Wonko also has a fishbowl.

It transpires that the world was saved from destruction by the dolphins, who somehow replaced it with an Earth from a parallel universe before making their farewells, leaving fishbowls as gifts.

Ford turns up, having escaped from the clutches of a Sirius Cybernetics Corporation rep, and sets off with Arthur and Fenchurch to see God's final message to His creation. On the way there, they discover Marvin, several times older than the universe and badly in need of repair. Together, the four travellers look on God's final message and are satisfied.

Background: Pan took a bold move with *So Long, and Thanks for All the Fish*, which was published as the company's first ever mass-market hardback. The shiny black dust jacket carried a small 'lenticular' picture stuck to the front. Often incorrectly described as a 'hologram', this was not a 3-D image but rather two completely different pictures. Viewed one way it showed a walrus, but tilted at an angle the image changed to a plesiosaur.

In 1988, the four *Hitchhiker's* paperbacks were republished by Pan in a uniform edition. The covers were divided into quarters so that four different images could be created, depending on how the books were arranged: a red and white 'Don't Panic' towel; a Babel fish; a painting of the *Heart of Gold* by acclaimed SF artist Chris Foss; and a computerised self-portrait of Douglas Adams. A mysterious pattern of coloured blobs on the books' spines revealed itself to be a colour-blindness test which showed the figure '42' – but not to everyone.

Comment: The most common reaction among *Hitchhiker's Guide* fans on reading *So Long, and Thanks for All the Fish* was: 'It's a bit slim, isn't it?' However nicely written it may be (and it is), however funny (it has some great moments), there simply isn't very much story. And a lot of what there is – Ford's solo adventures in trying to buy a drink, for example – seems somewhat superfluous to the main Arthur-Fenchurch story.

As the first entirely original *Hitchhiker's Guide* novel, *So Long* feels more naturally constructed than *Life, the Universe and Everything*, with a strong beginning, a satisfying middle and a wry if inconclusive ending. It's just a shame that the three of them are so close together. Zaphod and Trillian are mentioned, but don't appear, and Marvin's function is little more than a cameo to please the fans. Adams even steps outside his narrative at one point to suggest that the less patient readers should flick straight to the final chapter, 'which is a good bit and has Marvin in it.'

Nevertheless, the book succeeds admirably in terms of retrospectively explaining and connecting aspects of the earlier story which were constructed originally as little more than comic asides, and readers unaware of the books' disparate genesis could well believe that Adams planned this all from the start.

Young Zaphod Plays It Safe

Story: The Beeblebrox Salvage and Really Wild Stuff Corporation is employed by the Safety and Civil Reassurance Administration to track down a missing spaceship which should have delivered three deeply dangerous Sirius Cybernetics Corporation rejects into a black hole. The ship is found and one of the capsules is missing. The trajectory of the only escape pod is plotted and found to lead to a small planet in the sector ZZ9 Plural Z Alpha. The planet must be made 'perfectly safe' …

Background: In 1986, Douglas Adams became involved with the charity Comic Relief, for whom he co-edited with Peter Fincham a book of comedy material. Adams himself contributed three short stories to *The Utterly, Utterly Merry Comic Relief Christmas Book*, one and a half of which were *Hitchhiker's Guide* related.

The semi-*Hitchhiker's* story in the Comic Relief book was *The Private Life of Genghis Khan*, which Adams adapted from a TV sketch he had originally written with Graham Chapman in 1975. Adams added a cameo appearance by Wowbagger the Infinitely Prolonged, thus establishing the tale (in some people's view) as part of the *Hitchhiker's* canon. The third Douglas Adams' story in the book was *A Christmas Fairly Story*, co-written with Terry Jones. *The Private Life of Genghis Khan* was posted on Douglas Adams' official website some years later and is in early editions of *The Salmon of Doubt*, but *A Christmas Fairly Story* has never been reprinted.

Comment: *Young Zaphod Plays It Safe* remains the only absolutely 100 per cent *Hitchhiker's Guide* short story, although it left fans somewhat nonplussed, mainly because of the unclear ending. Just who was the mysterious being referred to at the story's close? Some people said it was (then US President) Ronald Reagan, while others maintained that it was Jesus Christ. When the story was eventually republished in Peter Haining's anthology *The Wizards of Odd* in 1996, the final line was changed to make it clear that the being is in fact Reagan, although the joke had by then of course lost all its topicality.

Mostly Harmless

Hardback: Heinemann, October 1992
Paperback: Pan Books, October 1993

Story: Tricia McMillan, a successful TV journalist, regrets not having gone off with the 'guy from another planet' whom she once met at a party, so she is happy to accompany three aliens who invite her back to their home world, Rupert, the solar system's tenth planet.

Sneaking into *The Hitchhiker's Guide to the Galaxy* offices, Ford Prefect reprograms a security robot to be his happy servant. Ford learns that the new management, InfiniDim Enterprises, want to boost profits by spreading a multidimensional *Hitchhiker's Guide* across infinite universes and by marketing the new version at affluent businessmen. He knocks out the editor, steals his ID card, and reprograms the main *Hitchhiker's Guide* computer.

Arthur Dent travels listlessly and recklessly, having lost Fenchurch in a hyperspace accident but knowing he can never die until after he has been to Stavromula Beta.

Ford discovers that the *Hitchhiker's Guide* offices have a secret thirteenth floor, on which he finds the *Hitchhiker's Guide* Mk 2, a smooth, circular, buttonless black device. He also realises that InfiniDim is run by Vogons. To safeguard the prototype *Hitchhiker's Guide* Mk 2, he sends it to Arthur.

Arthur has finally found peace as a sandwich maker on the planet of the Perfectly Normal Beasts. Much to his surprise he is visited by Trillian, now a successful intergalactic journalist, and her teenage daughter, Random, conceived using Arthur's DNA from a sperm bank. Trillian leaves Arthur and Random to get to know each other.

Random opens the package which Arthur receives; the *Hitchhiker's Guide* Mk 2 explains to her about probabilities and parallel universes and shows her an alternative version of her mother arriving on Rupert. Random takes off in a spaceship. Searching for her, Arthur finds Ford, whose ship it was, and they follow the migrating Perfectly Normal Beasts through a dimensional portal to the Domain of the King.

Back on Earth, Tricia McMillan is very surprised when

a teenage daughter she didn't know she had turns up in a spaceship. At the Domain of the King Bar and Grill, Arthur and Ford are given a spaceship by a singer and head to Earth, where they try to track down Tricia and Random, while the Vogons close in on the planet to finish a job they once started ...

Background: With the fifth book in 'the increasingly inaccurately named *Hitchhiker's Trilogy*', Douglas Adams' inability to hit deadlines really came to the fore. In January 1991, his new hardback publishers Heinemann announced that *Mostly Harmless* would be published in October of that year. In October they announced that the book would in fact be published in January 1992. By January the book remained unfinished and publication was rescheduled again, this time for July.

In March 1992 Heinemann resorted to literally locking Douglas Adams in a hotel room until he finished the damn book. This was too late for a July publication, so the date was set at October 1992, when the book finally appeared, exactly one year late.

Comment: *Mostly Harmless* reads even less like a *Hitchhiker's Guide* novel than *Life, the Universe and Everything*. It is far more serious than the previous four and deals with weightier subjects in terms of parallel universes, yet it also lacks the grand, pangalactic conceits of the original story. In early *Hitchhiker's Guide*, Arthur was a hapless witness to the insanity around him, while Ford, Zaphod, Trillian and Marvin hurtled around the universe, improbably interacting with things.

But *Mostly Harmless* is Arthur's personal story, along with the story of Trillian and Random. Trillian was never a fully fleshed out character, but comes into her own here – in both versions of herself. Random just about manages to avoid being a stereotypical teenager.

The book suffers by alternating too frequently for too long between the three subplots – Arthur, Tricia McMillan and Ford – before they all bind together at the end. If anything, this book is most notable for Adams' updated version of *Hitchhiker's Guide* itself, which reflects his growing interest in communication technology.

Incidentally, the idea that, when Zaphod first met Trillian at a fancy dress party, his second head was disguised as a parrot in a covered cage, originated in the computer game. Zaphod does not actually appear in this book, nor do Marvin, Slartibartfast, Fenchurch or any of the other expected characters. There is, however, a teasingly slight reference to 42.

5. The Recordings

The Hitchhiker's Guide to the Galaxy

Double LP or Double Cassette: Original Records, November 1979 (mail order), May 1980 (shops)

Cast: Peter Jones, Simon Jones, Geoffrey McGivern, Mark Wing-Davey, Cindy Oswin, Stephen Moore, Richard Vernon, Valentine Dyall, David Tate, Jim Broadbent, Bill Wallis

Story: The storyline of the double album approximately followed the first four episodes of the radio series, but with a few scenes deleted (for example, persuading Mr Prosser to lie in the mud) and other minor textual changes.

Background: 'We spoke to a couple of record companies after BBC Enterprises turned us down,' remembered producer Geoffrey Perkins. 'We agreed, in principle, to make a record with one guy who, while we were considering the contract, insisted on showing us a hardcore porn film.'

In the end, a deal was signed with Original Records, a

small independent label specialising in spoken word and comedy. The principal radio cast were reassembled with the exception of Susan Sheridan, who was working on the Disney film *The Black Cauldron*. Instead, Cindy Oswin from the ICA stage production was drafted in to play Trillian.

The album was first made available by mail order only, although it was later released to record shops. However, by then most *Hitchhiker's Guide* fans had ordered the album, so sales were poor. *The Hitchhiker's Guide to the Galaxy* is possibly the best-selling record never to make the charts.

After the first batch of records and tapes had been produced, an old school friend of Douglas Adams' complained about the name given to the worst poet in the universe. Rather than bring back Peter Jones to record four words, Original Records simply cut up that part of the master tape and reassembled it in the wrong order, resulting in the garbled nonsense which has puzzled listeners ever since.

Comment: In retrospect, BBC Records' decision to pass up the chance to release *Hitchhiker's Guide* has a certain logic to it. As a six-part serial, it would have required three LPs, an enormous investment in something which, though popular, had yet to prove its longevity (the double cassette format for radio comedy was still unknown at this time).

Geoffrey Perkins summed up the differences between the album and the radio series when he said, 'The radio series had been very low-tech, whereas the records were slightly more high-tech, which meant that on the one hand we could do a few more things that we wanted, but possibly the show lost something because of it. But there were some great things about the records, such as Tim Souster's music, which was extraordinary.'

The Hitchhiker's Guide to the Galaxy Part Two – The Restaurant at the End of the Universe

LP or Cassette: Original Records, November 1980

Cast: Peter Jones, Simon Jones, Geoffrey McGivern, Mark Wing-Davey, Cindy Oswin, Stephen Moore, Roy Hudd, Anthony Sharp, David Tate, Frank Middlemass, Stephen Grief, Loueen Willoughby, Graham de Wilde

Story: Ostensibly based on 'Fit the Fifth' and 'Fit the Sixth', the inclusion of the Disaster Area storyline in place of the Haggunenon sequence actually made the two sides of this album more similar to the TV series' episodes five and six (which were yet to be filmed). Whereas the previous album had cut about five minutes out of each episode's script, the second LP managed to actually be slightly longer than the two radio episodes on which it was based.

Background: One year later, the cast were reassembled to record a follow-up album. This reached number 47 in the charts but, despite massive promotion, it only sold as many as the barely promoted first album. Original Records ran into serious financial problems and were forcibly closed down when Douglas Adams took out a lawsuit against them, with all rights to the two albums given to Ed Victor Ltd in lieu of royalties. An American release was arranged through Harmony Records but neither album has been available since 1988 and there remains little chance of their ever being reissued.

Comment: For some reason, *The Restaurant at the End of the Universe* just doesn't have the same sparkle as the first album. It is too long and, being a follow-up, doesn't work on its own. However, at the time it looked unlikely that the radio series would ever be released so this was the only way to own the story in audio form. The album's poor reputation probably has more to do with its ubiquity in £1.99 remainder bins throughout the 1980s than its actual quality.

The Theme Single

Seven-inch single: Original Records, January 1981

Most of the music on the two Original Records' albums was written and recorded by Tim Souster, although Paddy Kingsland (who oversaw the music in the first series and composed the music for the second) also contributed a few tracks. Souster also recorded a new version of the *Hitchhiker's Guide* theme *Journey of the Sorcerer*, originally a track on the Eagles album *One of These Nights*.

Two of the three tracks on the B-side of this single were from *The Restaurant at the End of the Universe*: *Reg Nullify in Concert*, a song by Graham de Wilde heard in the background at Milliways; and Peter Jones' narration on the rock band Disaster Area, without Souster's backing music. What really excited the fans, however, was the final track, *Only the End of the World Again* by Disaster Area, a completely new sci-fi rock song featuring Douglas Adams himself on rhythm guitar.

When the BBC was unable to use the original Eagles track as theme music to the TV series (as they had done on radio) they licensed the Tim Souster version from Original Records.

The Marvin Singles

Marvin / Metal Man, Seven-inch single: Polydor, June 1981
Reasons to Be Miserable / Marvin I Love You, Seven-inch single: Depressive Discs/Polydor, October 1981

The man behind these singles was John Sinclair, producer of hit records for every band from Foreigner to Buggles, and an old friend of Stephen Moore.

'He was very much into what he called "the theatre of wax" which meant doing dramatic things on record, with music,' recalled Moore. 'We did it and we were happy with it, and we said, "Look, we can't not involve Douglas." So Douglas came round and he had lots of ideas – which we listened to very politely. Then we said, "Thanks. We'll put your name on the credits anyway, if that's all right with you." And he was quite happy with that.'

Marvin was released just as *Hitchhiker's Guide* fever was at its peak, with the TV series and the radio series both being repeated and *The Restaurant at the End of the Universe* still selling well. Promoted on radio and television, it reached number 53 in the charts, enough to make Marvin the only robot in *The Guinness Book of British Hit Singles*.

As a follow-up, Moore and Sinclair recorded two further songs – released as *The Double B-Side* – again giving an honorary credit to Adams. But public interest in *Hitchhiker's Guide* was by now on the wane. The record failed to make the top 75 and rapidly became a collector's item. What has remained largely unknown is that Moore and Sinclair recorded a third Marvin single, a Christmas song. However, the failure of *The Double B-Side* resulted in Polydor losing interest in the project and the single never even made it as far as a final mix. It is unlikely that this will ever be heard because the copyright situation after all this time will be extremely complex.

The Abridged Talking Books

The Hitchhiker's Guide to the Galaxy, Double Cassette: Listen for Pleasure, November 1981

The Restaurant at the End of the Universe, Double Cassette: Listen for Pleasure, April 1983

Life, the Universe and Everything, Double Cassette: Listen for Pleasure, October 1984

So Long, and Thanks for All the Fish, Double Cassette: Listen for Pleasure, September 1985

Background: Talking Books were just starting to become popular in the early 1980s when Listen for Pleasure, a budget label owned by EMI, released the four (as was) *Hitchhiker's Guide* novels. Four books in this format by one author was unprecedented and the tapes

HITCHHIKER'S GUIDE

sold incredibly well, only being deleted in the early 1990s
when they were supplanted by unabridged readings.
Producer Barry McCann abridged the text of each book
to a running time of approximately two hours. Stephen
Moore tried where he could to match the voices of the
characters as they had been on the radio.

Comment: Although the unabridged readings have since
supplanted these ones, they are still worth listening to.
Moore is an excellent reader and the abridgements are
sensitive and well done.

The Unabridged Talking Books

The Hitchhiker's Guide to the Galaxy, Four Cassettes: Isis
Audio Books, April 1994, Four CDs: Isis Audio Books,
November 1994, Four Cassettes or Five CDs: BBC
Word for Word, November 2002

The Restaurant at the End of the Universe, Four Cassettes: Isis
Audio Books, April 1994, Four Cassettes or Five CDs:
BBC Word for Word, November 2002

Life, the Universe and Everything, Four Cassettes: Isis Audio
Books, May 1994, Four Cassettes or Five CDs: BBC
Word for Word, November 2002

So Long, and Thanks for All the Fish, Four Cassettes: Isis
Audio Books, May 1994, Four Cassettes or Five CDs:
BBC Word for Word, November 2002

Mostly Harmless, Four Cassettes: Isis Audio Books, June
1994, Four Cassettes or Five CDs: BBC Word for Word,
November 2002

Background: Dove Audio, one of the leading producers of spoken word recordings in the USA, acquired the rights to *The Hitchhiker's Guide to the Galaxy* and its sequels in 1990 and asked Douglas Adams himself to read them. The results ran to approximately six hours each and were spread over four cassettes per book. In 1994, Isis Audio Books acquired the UK rights to these recordings, releasing them singly and as a five-book, 20-cassette pack.

Comment: With his experience of performing in Footlights, Douglas Adams had no problem in providing dramatic readings of his own works. These can be regarded as the definitive readings, and the first was even nominated for a Grammy. Curiously, although recorded for an American company, the readings match the British editions.

The Hitchhiker's Guide to the Galaxy broke new ground yet again when it became the first unabridged audio book to be released on compact disc, initially in a signed limited edition of 1,600. Unfortunately, *The Restaurant at the End of the Universe* is a slightly longer book and simply could not be fitted onto four CDs. Isis were reluctant to edit the recording, but were equally unhappy about releasing it as five discs. BBC Worldwide, when they acquired the rights, had no such qualms.

In 2005, a second unabridged audiobook of the first novel was released, read by Stephen Fry.

The Radio Series

Ten years after it was broadcast, and with the Original Records' versions deleted, the BBC finally released the original radio series of *Hitchhiker's Guide* in September 1988. It was available as a boxed set of either six cassettes or six compact discs, the first BBC radio programme to be released in CD format.

There was one minor cut in the programme, in 'Fit the Third' when Marvin hums *Shine on You Crazy Diamond* by Pink Floyd, as the BBC was unable to obtain permission to use the song. All the other music used in the first series, by artists such as Jean-Michel Jarre and Tomita, was cleared for release, including the Eagles' version of *Journey of the Sorcerer* and the traditional closing theme, Louis Armstrong singing *What a Wonderful World*.

In 1993 the series was re-released as two double-cassettes with series one renamed *The Primary Phase* and 'Fit the Seventh' plus series two called *The Secondary Phase*. CD reissues under these titles appeared in 1997 as two three-disc packs, and the tapes were reissued again in new packaging in March 1998 to mark the show's twentieth anniversary.

All 12 episodes (plus a radio documentary and Douglas Adams interview) were collected together in October 2001 on an eight-disc set, *The Hitchhiker's Guide to the Galaxy: The Collector's Edition*. Since this was both expensive and heavy, the same material was released as *The Complete Hitchhiker's Guide to the Galaxy* on a single disc in MP3 format (once again setting a precedent for BBC material). However, the quality of the MP3 version is reported to be very poor.

Douglas Adams at the BBC

Three CDs: BBC Worldwide, 2004

Based on an idea by the author of this very book, this three-CD set collects together dozens of interviews, sketches, etc. either written by or featuring Douglas Adams. The oldest items are Adams-penned sketches from the BBC broadcast of the 1974 Cambridge Footlights Revue and the 1974 Radio 4 series *Oh No, It Isn't*. Also included are the three sketches which Adams wrote for *The Burkiss Way* in 1977 and the 'Sheila's Ear' mini-episode of *Hitchhiker's Guide*. His work on *Doctor Who* is represented by extracts from *The Pirate Planet* and Tom Baker can also be heard in clips from *Hyperland*.

There are numerous extracts from the radio series of *Last Chance to See* and Adams' two later radio series, *The Hitchhiker's Guide to the Future* and *The Internet: The Last 20th Century Battleground*, as well as the posthumous TV and radio tribute programmes which were produced in late 2001. Miscellaneous radio and TV appearances by Douglas Adams include *Desert Island Discs*, *Have I Got News for You* and *Quote … Unquote*.

The whole 'programme' (all three and three-quarter hours of it) was written and researched by physicist-turned-comedy actor Chris Emmett, produced by the *Tertiary Phase*'s Dirk Maggs and narrated by Simon Jones. Probably the oddest item is a 1994 recording of Douglas Adams singing on Radio 2.

The Tertiary, Quandary and Quintessential Phases

Immediately after its broadcast in late 2004, *The Tertiary Phase* was released on three CDs. This version included about 20 minutes of additional material, scattered across the six episodes. Similarly expanded double-CD releases of the fourth and fifth series followed after they were broadcast in 2005. In May 2005 *The Tertiary Phase* became the first radio series to be released on DVD-Audio. This was expected to include a video documentary by Kevin Jon Davies, director of the TV series *Making of ...* documentary, who had shot hours of footage and interviews in the recording studio. Unfortunately the documentary never appeared and the DVD-A's only advantage over the CDs was that the show was mixed in 5.1 surround sound (which was a version that had already been broadcast over the web).

6. The Television Series

The BBC TV Series

Episode 1:

First broadcast: 5 January 1981

Cast: Peter Jones, Simon Jones, David Dixon, Joe Melia, Martin Benson, Steve Conway, Cleo Rocos, Andrew Mussell

Story: Arthur Dent finds that his house is about to be knocked down and learns that his friend Ford Prefect is an alien. Ford and Arthur escape from the Earth just as the Vogons blow it up, but are captured and threatened with poetry.

Episode 2:

First broadcast: 12 January 1981

Cast: Peter Jones, Simon Jones, David Dixon, Mark Wing-Davey, Sandra Dickinson, Stephen Moore, David Learner, Martin Benson, Michael Cule, David Tate, Rayner Bourton, Gil Morris

Story: Arthur and Ford are subjected to Vogon poetry, then thrown into space where they are rescued by the *Heart of Gold*, on board which they find the improbable crew of Zaphod Beeblebrox, Trillian and Marvin.

Episode 3:

First broadcast: 19 January 1981

Cast: Peter Jones, Simon Jones, David Dixon, Mark Wing-Davey, Sandra Dickinson, Stephen Moore, David Learner, David Tate, Richard Vernon

Story: In orbit around Magrathea, Arthur saves the day by improbably turning two missiles into a bowl of petunias and a whale. On the planet, Ford, Arthur and Trillian explore underground, while Arthur and Marvin stay on the surface. Arthur meets Slartibartfast, who shows him the Earth Mk 2.

Episode 4:

First broadcast: 26 January 1981

Cast: Peter Jones, Simon Jones, David Dixon, Mark Wing-Davey, Sandra Dickinson, Richard Vernon, Anthony Carrick, Timothy Davies, David Leland, Charles McKeown, Marc Smith, Valentine Dyall

Story: Arthur watches recordings of the day Deep Thought was switched on and the day it proclaimed the answer to life, the universe and everything to be 42, and he learns about the origins of the Earth. Trillian's mice want to dissect Arthur's brain but the cops arrive searching for Zaphod and in the confusion Arthur, Ford, Zaphod and Trillian escape. They cower behind a computer bank, which explodes ...

Episode 5:

First broadcast: 2 February 1981

Cast: Peter Jones, Simon Jones, David Dixon, Mark Wing-Davey, Sandra Dickinson, Stephen Moore, David Learner, Peter Davison, Jack May, Colin Jeavons, Dave Prowse, Barry Frank Warren, Colin Bennett

Story: ... Depositing them at Milliways, which was built on the ancient ruins of Magrathea. Ford says 'hello' to Hotblack Desiato and Arthur is repulsed by the talking Dish of the Day. Marvin telephones them from the car park and they head down there, where they steal an extremely black spaceship. Unfortunately, it cannot be controlled from onboard and is programmed to fly into a star.

Episode 6:

First broadcast: 9 February 1981

Cast: Peter Jones, Simon Jones, David Dixon, Mark Wing-Davey, Sandra Dickinson, Stephen Moore, David

Learner, Rayner Bourton, Aubrey Morris, Beth Porter, Matthew Scurfield, David Neville, Geoffrey Beevers, David Rowlands, Jon Glover

Story: Marvin stays on board to allow Ford, Arthur, Zaphod and Trillian to escape by teleport. Ford and Arthur materialise on the Golgrafrinchan 'B' Ark which crashes into and colonises Fintlewoodlewix. Arthur and Ford recognise the planet as prehistoric Earth and realise that its programming is now flawed. Resigned to their fate, they wander off to explore the planet.

Background: As early as 1978, consideration was being given to a TV version of *Hitchhiker's Guide*, but the real starting point of the *Hitchhiker's Guide* TV series was a memo from John Lloyd to the BBC Head of Light Entertainment in September 1979. Lloyd would go on to be credited as Associate Producer on the series, although his work on the hugely successful *Not the Nine O'Clock News* meant that his input to the later episodes was minimal. He also received an Additional Material credit for Episode Five, relating back to his work on the original radio scripts.

The first task in producing the TV series was to appoint a producer. Alan JW Bell was a veteran of BBC TV sitcoms but with no experience in science fiction or the more surreal aspects of TV comedy. While his workman-like attitude and levelheadedness undoubtedly helped to bring the show in on schedule and within the budget, there was a definite clash of personalities between Bell and the Oxbridge young guns.

Bell received the pilot script in January 1980, around the same time that Adams was waxing enthusiastic to interviewers about the prospects of the animation which he envisaged as accompanying the narration sequences: 'What you can do just with computer diagrams and computer graphics is immensely exciting.'

Indeed it was, but it was also incredibly crude and blocky, making it difficult to get over the sort of subtle, throwaway visual gags that a series like *Hitchhiker's Guide* demanded. This was the era of the Acorn Atom and the ZX80 and smooth, scrolling computer animation was unknown to anyone without access to a Cray supercomputer.

The problem was solved by a chance meeting between Bell and a teenage animator. Kevin Jon Davies was already a massive fan of the series, and his enthusiasm not only persuaded Bell to take the producer's job, but also gave Davies' employer, Pearce Studios, the chance to bid for and win the opportunity to create the TV series' graphics.

It should be stressed at this point (and will be again) that *no computers were used in the creation of the TV series graphics*. The whole of every single animated sequence was created using traditional cel animation techniques, just like any cartoon. Not only do certain erroneous publications and ill-informed authors persist in spreading this myth, but occasionally unscrupulous computer graphics artists have even dishonestly claimed credit for the animation.

Although Peter Jones' narration was virtually identical to that used in the radio series, it was recorded anew. Animator Rod Lord and his team then printed out the text and accompanying graphical images in negative on plastic cels. Coloured gels were placed behind the cels which were photographed on a lightbox. Animation and text were made to gradually appear by placing a solid black cel on top and moving it slightly (one letter at a time) as each new frame was photographed.

Several of the radio cast were retained for the TV series, with Simon Jones and Mark Wing-Davey returning to the roles which had been based on them in the first place. However, Ford Prefect was recast from original actor (and inspiration) Geoffrey McGivern to David Dixon. American actress Sandra Dickinson, who was married at the time to the actor then playing Doctor Who, Peter Davison, took the role of Trillian. Stephen Moore was offered the chance to play Marvin, but elected to only supply the voice and so the costume was filled by David Learner, who had played the role on stage.

The only other two actors from the radio series to transfer to television in the same roles were Richard Vernon as Slartibartfast and David Tate as Eddie the computer. Valentine Dyall, the radio series' Gargravarr, provided the voice of Deep Thought as he had for the LP version, while Michael Cule, who had played numerous roles in the Rainbow Theatre production, achieved his aim of landing the Vogon Guard role.

Jim Francis, a veteran of *Blake's 7* and *Doctor Who*, was called on at short notice to design and build the many special effects required, including Zaphod's second head and the Marvin costume. The second head was given limited (radio-controlled) movement, but was generally held to be less than successful, more because of time constraints than budget, according to Francis. Mark Wing-

Davey was slightly aggrieved to discover that the head actually cost more than he did. Zaphod's third arm was either tucked, Napoleon-style, into the character's jacket or provided by effects technician Mike Kelt, standing behind Wing-Davey.

Cheap though the series looks in retrospect, it was actually extremely expensive, sapping almost the entire effects budget of the Light Entertainment department for 1980. One result of this was that the BBC could not afford to make a series of *The Goodies* that year, which precipitated that trio's move to London Weekend Television.

The pilot was recorded in May and June 1980. In order to persuade the BBC that it genuinely was funny, a screening was arranged at the National Film Theatre to which a hundred science fiction fans were invited, their response being added as a laughter track. For this screening, Peter Jones recorded a special introduction, his only on-screen appearance for *Hitchhiker's Guide* (later included on the DVD). The pilot episode received two other public preview screenings: at the Edinburgh Television Festival and at Hitchercon 1, the first ever *Hitchhiker's Guide to the Galaxy* convention.

With the BBC persuaded that the series could work, production on the remaining five episodes ran from September 1980 through to January 1981, with the final special effects footage for Episode Six being shot three days after the first episode went on air.

Locations used in the series included a clay pit in Cornwall as Magrathea and a hillside in Lancashire as Prehistoric Earth. Arthur's house and the nearby pub were both in Surrey. Most of the sets were constructed at

Television Centre in London, where the revolving stage from *Blankety Blank* was redressed to become the bridge of the *Heart of Gold*. The scenes featuring Deep Thought were shot at Ealing, while the explosion of a Magrathean computer bank was shot outside on a reconstructed set for safety reasons. Matte paintings were used to create the interior of the Vogon ship and the pier at Southend, while some of the Vogon corridors were redressed sets from the film *Alien*.

Although the series was finished on schedule, time constraints were very tight and several scenes were either not filmed or filmed but subsequently cut. One shot of Arthur Dent was actually spare footage of Simon Jones running across the studio to shoot another scene. One of the cut scenes involved Arthur finding a silver costume in his quarters on the *Heart of Gold* – although it is now accepted that Arthur spends the entire story dressed in his dressing gown and pyjamas, this was never actually stated in either the radio series or the first two novels.

First broadcast as six 35-minute episodes, the series was trimmed to fit a 30-minute slot from its first repeat and the excised scenes were only restored when the series was released on video in May 1992. This video release also added a very small amount of previously unseen footage, but removed all credits except the opening title sequence of Episode One and the closing credits of Episode Six.

Comment: Two decades on, the TV series of *Hitchhiker's Guide* still passes one crucial test – it's still funny. The cast are good and the script is witty. But it is the animated graphics which most people remember and which deservedly won the bulk of the series' acclaim. It says something about the animation's sophistication that many published sources mistakenly describe them as 'an early example of computer graphics' (it also says something about the amount of research that goes into some books on cult television). In actual fact, computer graphics in 1980 were still extremely primitive and even with the most sophisticated computers available (and a huge budget), the BBC could never have produced animation as smooth as this.

Where the series is let down, as many critics have observed, is in the special effects. The spaceships are crudely matted against the backgrounds; the wires supporting Slartibartfast's air-car are obvious; and Zaphod's second head is slightly less lifelike than Torchy the Battery Boy. But the series must be seen within its historical context. Effective, impressive science fiction special effects were limited at this time to Hollywood movies such as *Star Wars* and would not make inroads into television until several years later. When *The Hitchhiker's Guide to the Galaxy* was produced, even American television could not produce anything more impressive by way of special effects than *Battlestar Galactica* or *Buck Rogers in the 25th Century*. Given the minuscule resources of BBC TV, the effects on *Hitchhiker's Guide* were, if not better, at least better value for money.

The design work in the TV series met with mixed reactions, and still does. Stephen Moore disliked the Marvin costume and declined to wear it, leaving a vacancy for David Learner to recreate his role from the stage production. But as Visual Effects Designer Jim Francis observed: 'One of the hardest people to please was Douglas Adams. He'd never really visualised what the *Heart of Gold* looked like, what Marvin looked like, or anything looked like. It was all just in words. But when you put something in front of him, he'd just go, "No, it's not like that, that's not how I see it."'

The Making of The Hitchhiker's Guide to the Galaxy

The importance of Kevin Jon Davies in the history of *Hitchhiker's Guide* cannot be understated. He was directly responsible for Pearce Studios providing the TV series' animated graphics, and later oversaw the creation of *The Illustrated Hitchhiker's Guide to the Galaxy*. In-between, he produced *The Making of The Hitchhiker's Guide to the Galaxy* for BBC video.

Being a massive fan of *Hitchhiker's Guide* since the radio version, Davies took advantage of his access to the set of the TV series, on the second half of which he was actually given a series of spoof credits: 'Mouse Trainer', 'Milliways Catering' and 'Bath Superintendent.' Davies took many photographs on the set and even shot some home video footage.

In 1992, he persuaded BBC Enterprises that this unseen footage could be incorporated into a documentary about the making of the TV series. Interviews with Douglas Adams and others were shot in October of that year, together with new dramatised scenes filmed on location at 'Arthur Dent's house' in Sussex. Simon Jones,

David Dixon and Mike Cule recreated their roles for the documentary, and the original Marvin costume was located and used. Although it sold well on video (including an American release), *The Making of The Hitchhiker's Guide to the Galaxy* has never been broadcast on television.

The Second Television Series

When the TV version of *Hitchhiker's Guide* proved to be a success, the obvious question raised was whether there would be a second series. Mark Wing-Davey said in an interview that the second series would start at a cricket match, suggesting that Douglas Adams was considering basing the script on his unused *Doctor Who* treatment, *Doctor Who and the Krikkitmen*.

However, the complexities and expense of the first series meant that a second series was deemed non-viable and it was confirmed cancelled in November 1981, just as publication of a third novel was announced.

Geoffrey Perkins summed up the problems when he said, 'I was asked to be script editor of the putative second TV series, but I turned it down on the grounds that the absolutely worst job in the world was trying to get a script out of Douglas.'

The DVD

In late 2001 *The Hitchhiker's Guide to the Galaxy* came to DVD in a superb two-disc package. The six separate episodes were presented in the best – and longest –

versions possible, making the DVD version more complete than either the VHS release or the broadcast version. Rather than a commentary track, detailed on-screen notes were provided by Kevin Jon Davies which are as entertaining as they are informative. The complete *Making of the Hitchhiker's Guide* was included along with an additional half-hour of similar material which had been cut from the documentary before its original release. Other extras included a piece on the recording of the radio series from a schools programme and a deleted scene as well as some hidden 'Easter Eggs'.

The American DVD release included all the above as well as the 2001 tribute programme *Omnibus: Douglas Adams – The Man Who Blew Up the World*.

The Big Read

The Big Read was a 2003 BBC series which aimed to find the nation's favourite novel. The top 20 from an open vote were each given a half-hour programme fronted by a celebrity. In the case of *Hitchhiker's Guide* this was comedian Sanjeev Bhaskar, who took the opportunity to play Arthur Dent in a series of dramatised excerpts from the book.

An absolutely extraordinary cast included Roger Lloyd Pack (*Only Fools and Horses*) as Slartibartfast, Nigel Planer (*The Young Ones*) as the voice of Marvin, Sir Patrick Moore as The Book and Professor Stephen Hawking as Deep Thought. The programme was produced and directed by Deep Sehgal.

In the final voting, *Hitchhiker's Guide* came fourth,

beaten only by *Pride and Prejudice*, Philip Pulman's *His Dark Materials* trilogy and the overall winner, *Lord of the Rings*.

7. Other Versions of The Hitchhiker's Guide to the Galaxy

The Computer Game

Story: The storyline of the *Hitchhiker's Guide* computer game starts out, as in previous versions, with Arthur Dent (the player) waking up to find his house about to be knocked down, then being rescued by Ford Prefect just before the Earth goes the same way. However, later on the story diverged extensively from that of the books, TV series or radio series, with not only old favourites such as Zaphod, Marvin and Trillian but also a host of new characters, situations and ideas.

One notable innovation was that the computer, on occasions, lied to the player, telling him things were in one place when they were in fact somewhere else. Another radical idea was that the player did not necessarily remain as Arthur all the way through the game. Frustrated players, who found themselves resorting to violence in an attempt to get information out of Ford Prefect, in one scene were alarmed to find that later in the game they had become Ford in that same scene, at which point they had no choice but to suffer the abuse which they had previously meted out.

Background: With the tremendous popularity of *The Hitchhiker's Guide to the Galaxy* in the 1980s, it was almost inevitable that the concept would be turned into a computer game. However, game graphics of that era were largely limited to crudely drawn, heavily pixelated characters with limited animation running around two-dimensional environments, and to follow that route would have been a great disservice to *Hitchhiker's Guide*.

Douglas Adams was a fan of the games produced by a company called Infocom, which were text-only adventures dubbed 'interactive fiction'. The setting, characters and events were all described as in a book, with the player typing instructions to determine (hopefully) the course of events. Other companies also produced text-only adventures, but Infocom were the world leaders, not least because of their state-of-the-art programming, which allowed the games to recognise sentence structure and therefore respond more realistically to instructions.

In 1983 Adams approached Infocom (whose biggest hits up till then had been *Zork* and its sequels) with the idea of a *Hitchhiker's Guide* computer game. He was paired with Steve Meretzky, an Infocom programmer who had not only won awards for his games *Planetfall* and *Sorcerer*, but was also a long-time fan of *Hitchhiker's Guide*. In an early example of e-commerce, the two collaborated by swapping ideas across the Atlantic through modems.

Released on a 5.25 inch floppy disk, *The Hitchhiker's Guide to the Galaxy* was lavishly packaged, with a pair of (cardboard) Joo Janta peril-sensitive sunglasses (as worn by Zaphod Beeblebrox, and designed to prevent the wearer from seeing anything which might alarm them); demolition orders for Arthur Dent's house (in English) and the Earth (in Vogon); a 'Don't Panic' button badge; a microscopic space fleet (effectively an empty polythene sachet); a sales brochure for the *Hitchhiker's Guide*; and a packet of fluff. The game itself offered three different levels of text: 'brief', 'super-brief' and 'verbose' – the last of which offered as much text as a reasonably sized novel.

For those players who became completely stumped by the game, an 'invisiclues' hints book could be ordered from Infocom, in which suggestions could be revealed by the use of a special pen.

Comment: *The Hitchhiker's Guide to the Galaxy* was a huge hit with both public and critics, on both sides of the Atlantic, when it was released in late 1984. It was the first time that a major author had been directly involved in the creation of a computer game, and there was extensive adulatory press coverage.

As a follow-up, Adams created a totally original game for Infocom called *Bureaucracy*, an epic quest to get a bank to acknowledge a change of address card. This was partly written by Michael Bywater. 'Infocom was in the midst of some of the problems which eventually led to their demise at the time,' recalled Adams, 'and the project kept stopping and starting. Most of the initial work on *Bureaucracy* was mine, but in the end I was less involved with it than I was with the *HHGG* game.'

Both games were released on CD-ROM, together with other titles, in 1994 as *The Lost Treasures of Infocom Vols 1* and *2*. An on-line version of *The Hitchhiker's Guide to the Galaxy* was subsequently made available by The Digital

Village in conjunction with Comic Relief. In 2004 a version appeared on the BBC's *Hitchhiker's Guide* website, simultaneously with the start of *The Tertiary Phase*, which featured illustrations by Rod Lord, who had provided the TV series graphics.

The Other Computer Game

Story: Rescued from the destruction of Earth, Arthur Dent must face a series of trials, armed only with his trusty towel. If he passes all the tests, the Towelin Monks will present him with a special towel which will be sufficient to defeat the Krikkit Robots. Along the way, Arthur meets Ford, Zaphod, Trillian, Marvin, Slartibartfast, Thor, the Vogons, the Dentrassi, some mice in robotic exo-sketelons and the Ravenous Bugblatter Beast of Traal.

Background: In 1998, Douglas Adams' company The Digital Village announced that it was working on a new *Hitchhiker's Guide* computer game which would be 'an action-adventure game involving cricket, tea, petunias and very long lunches.' It was intended for release in 2000, simultaneously with the film.

The game was officially launched at the E3 conference in 2001, a few weeks after Adams' death, although at that stage it was still little more than a few clips of Arthur Dent running down corridors. In January 2002, with very little warning, the project was cancelled by the Swedish company which had financed it.

Comment: Hopes were high for this game. Douglas

Adams was heavily involved in developing the story – in fact, this was the last version of *Hitchhiker's Guide* on which he worked – and the promise of 'new' *Hitchhiker's* adventures was tantalising. The backers' decision to pull the plug seems to have been purely a financial one and it is impossible to say how justified that was.

A selection of characters and locations from the game are available to view on the Planet Magrathea website.

The Illustrated Hitchhiker's Guide to the Galaxy

Hardback: Weidenfeld and Nicolson, 1994

Cast: Jonathan Lermit, Tom Finnis, Francis Johnson, Michael Cule, Janos Kuruz

Story: The text of *The Illustrated Hitchhiker's Guide to the Galaxy* exactly matches that of the ordinary published novel, with one tiny change. The novel describes Zaphod as having long, blond hair, so a footnote was added to explain why he might appear – to some people – to have short, dark hair.

Background: It was in July 1993 that Douglas Adams came up with the concept of *The Illustrated Hitchhiker's Guide to the Galaxy*, using computer-based technology to combine sets, props and actors into fabulous photographic images. To oversee the project – dubbed 'the movie that doesn't move' – Adams suggested Kevin Jon Davies, who had worked on the TV series graphics and the *Making of The Hitchhiker's Guide to the Galaxy* video.

To generate interest, a test photograph was taken for display at the Frankfurt Book Fair. Martin Bower, a veteran of shows such as *Space: 1999*, built a very impressive Vogon constructor ship, incorporating an asteroid on a chain for smashing planets, plus the *Hitchhiker's Guide* itself and Ford Prefect's electronic thumb.

David Dixon and Simon Jones, the TV series' Ford and Arthur, were approached to pose in the scene, which showed Ford and Arthur standing on the rubble of Arthur's cottage, threatened by a bulldozer, while the Vogon ship roared overhead. However, Jones was unavailable and so Alistair Lock (whom Davies knew from a fan-produced *Doctor Who* spoof, *The Few Doctors*) stood in. This photograph was not used in the book but was published later in *SFX* magazine.

Response at Frankfurt was good, so a full set of images was commissioned. Davies sketched out the scenes which he felt would be most interesting, many of which were extremely peripheral to the plot. A new Ford and Arthur were cast, together with other characters, although no one was needed to play Marvin, a skeletal design which very obviously contained no actor (this also meant that it could be built at a cost effective half-size and still appear six feet tall when matted into the pictures).

All the cast were actors except for Tali, who was a model. Davies himself cameoed as the bulldozer driver, while galactic cops Shooty and Bang Bang were played by Douglas Adams and his agent Ed Victor.

Comment: *The Illustrated Hitchhiker's Guide to the Galaxy* is an absolutely gorgeous folly which was the victim of the publishers' uncertainty and a vicious circle of retail. Weidenfeld and Nicolson published a lavish volume with an unusually high price; many potential buyers cooed over it in the shops, and vowed to buy it the moment it was remaindered; because they didn't buy it, it was remaindered, and then they bought it, but by then it was too late.

In retrospect, the publishers would have been better advised to produce a cheaper standard edition and a really OTT drop-dead fabulous collector's edition at a higher price. But retrospect is easy and nobody could have predicted how this unique book would sell.

The designs are simply stunning, far better than anything in the TV series or the comics. There are many surprises and visual jokes hidden away in the backgrounds, including some props from other TV shows to delight hardcore science fiction fans. There is also fun to be had in realising precisely which parts of the text are being alluded to, because in many cases – the Arcturan mega-donkey, the pencil floating across the *Heart of Gold* bridge – they are far from the obvious ones.

Ironically, time has not been kind to *The Illustrated Hitchhiker's Guide to the Galaxy*. Image manipulation by computer has developed so fast that what caused gasps of incredulity in 1994 is now seen as commonplace. The visual style of the images remains, but the technological thrill of their construction has faded with alarming speed.

Unfortunately, many fans baulked at paying £25 (or, in America, $42!) for a novel they already owned, however beautifully produced. Sales were poor, and the book was eventually remaindered. Eventually, all stocks were acquired by Douglas Adams and signed copies are still available through www.douglasadams.com.

The Comics

Background: In 1992 sample artwork was circulated showing Arthur, Ford, Zaphod, Trillian, Marvin and Prostetnic Vogon Jeltz as they were to appear in DC Comics' adaptation of *The Hitchhiker's Guide to the Galaxy*. The three-issue series was a straightforward adaptation of the first novel by John Carnell, with artwork by Steve Leialoha, a British ex-patriot based in Hawaii.

Douglas Adams' only involvement with the comics was his vetoing of any textual changes and his approval of the character designs, although this took some time. The comics eventually appeared in late 1993, exactly one year late.

One year later, Carnell and Leialoha (with inker Shepherd Hendrix) produced a three-part adaptation of *The Restaurant at the End of the Universe*. A series of 100 *Hitchhiker's Guide* trading cards was also available at this time, distributed by CARDZ Inc., with artwork based on that in the comics. The cards were sold in sealed packs of eight, with randomly inserted 'chase' cards signed by Douglas Adams.

A three-issue comic adaptation of *Life, the Universe and Everything* followed in 1996. Then in 1997 the *Hitchhiker's Guide* comics were collected into a graphic novel, which also included an introduction by Adams and a selection of art from the trading cards. However, the comic-book versions of the second and third novels have yet to receive this treatment.

Comment: Many *Hitchhiker's Guide* fans found the comics to be a crushing disappointment. With the feature film stuck in development hell, this was an opportunity to present the story in a visual medium, unhampered by effects budgets or interfering Hollywood executives. Yet the published comics completely failed to use the medium's potential to reinvent the story, as other versions had done. Instead, they simply retold the novel in a heavily abridged form through some lacklustre artwork.

The comics are a largely forgettable footnote in the *Hitchhiker's Guide* canon, of interest only to completists. Douglas Adams' lack of interest in the medium or involvement in the project is summed up by his response to a query about the comics on his website a few years later: 'I don't know what DC published or didn't publish in the end.'

8. Documenting The Hitchhiker's Guide to the Galaxy

Don't Panic

Paperback: Titan Books, 1988
Paperback (revised): Titan Books, 1993
Paperback (revised): Titan Books, 2002

Background: Prior to this one, there had only been one book published about *The Hitchhiker's Guide to the Galaxy*, which is remarkable given the popularity of the series and how many books there are on other cult sci-fi and/or comedy shows. And like the subject it covered, Neil Gaiman's *Don't Panic* had a long and complex history. Originally conceived in 1979 by Stan Nicholls, manager of London sci-fi shop Forbidden Planet and now a successful author in his own right; the project was revived several years later. Neil Gaiman was then a struggling journalist and comics writer who had compiled (with film critic Kim Newman) a book about bad horror and sci-fi.

'I did several interviews with Douglas Adams as a young journalist in 1983–'84,' he said, 'or I may have only done one interview and sold it to lots of places – I forget. Anyway, in 1986 Titan Books had the licence to do a

Hitchhiker's companion, but they mislaid the writer they had. Titan asked Kim Newman, who didn't want to do it but suggested me. And I said sure. I enjoyed interviewing all the people I needed to talk to and spending time going through Douglas' filing cabinets.'

An American edition of *Don't Panic* was published shortly after the British one and a German translation the following year. When the book was updated in 1993 (one year late!), Gaiman was a big name in comics and the new material was written instead by his friend David K Dickson. A third edition in 2002 was revised and updated by MJ Simpson.

Comment: *Don't Panic* is packed with goodies, including unused material from the radio and TV scripts, a partial synopsis of *Doctor Who and the Krikkitmen*, and a facsimile of Douglas Adams' original four-page treatment for *The Hitchhiker's Guide to the Galaxy*. What it doesn't have is any pictures. 'We had a great set of illustrations for it,' lamented Gaiman, 'but the publishers decided at the last minute that they weren't going to go with them.'

Gaiman's style is light and chatty yet informative and enthusiastic, although occasionally it strays a little too much into *faux* Douglas Adams. The third edition was rather cheekily promoted as a 'biography' of Douglas Adams, which was not strictly true.

Hitchhiker: A Biography of Douglas Adams

Hardback: Hodder & Stoughton, 2003
Paperback (revised): Coronet, 2003

Background: The first full-length biography of Douglas Adams was commissioned a few months after his death in 2001 and published on the 25th anniversary of the original radio series. *Hitchhiker's Guide* expert MJ Simpson interviewed more than 90 of Adams' friends and colleagues for the book, which also drew on 200 published and broadcast interviews, as well as extensive research into the archives of Brentwood School, the Cambridge Footlights and the BBC. John Lloyd, co-writer of two *Hitchhiker's* episodes and *The Meaning of Liff*, provided the foreword for the UK edition, replaced in the American edition with a foreword by Neil Gaiman.

Comment: The recurring theme in *Hitchhiker* is the debunking of popular myths surrounding Douglas Adams, many of them repeated by Adams himself in interviews. Previously undocumented elements of his career are described, such as his work on the *Labyrinth* computer game, and stories which have been largely glossed over are explored in detail, notably the unfortunate situation surrounding the LP versions.

Astute readers will have spotted that the author of this book also wrote *Hitchhiker*, so I can offer only other people's critical comments: *Publisher's Weekly* called *Hitchhiker* 'a must-have for serious Adams fans', *Literary Review* said it was 'a fine epitaph' and the American Library Association called it 'a biography that will entertain die-hard fans and those who've never cracked a *Hitchhiker* book alike.'

The text of the British paperback was revised and updated, while the American hardback included a new introduction and explanatory notes on the finer points of British popular culture. The American paperback added an afterword, recounting events after Adams' death. Consequently all four Englsh language editions are slightly different.

Wish You Were Here: The Official Biography of Douglas Adams

Hardback: Hodder Headline, 2003
Paperback: Hodder Headline, 2004

Background: When the contract for *Hitchhiker* was signed in 2001, the Douglas Adams estate maintained that there were absolutely no plans for an official, authorised biography – but one was announced less than two months later. The author was Nick Webb, the one-time junior editor at Pan Books who had signed Adams to novelise his radio scripts in 1978. Although he had not worked with Adams since then, the two had stayed friends.

Comment: Webb's book is more of a personal remembrance of Douglas Adams than a definitive biography. The author's background shows through in that the sections on publishing are very detailed while parts of the book dealing with broadcasting, film and computer games are weaker. Webb had access to Adams' somewhat disordered personal files, but unfortunately he repeats several stories which are now known to be merely the products of the subject's overactive imagination. And for a book written by a former editor, there are a surprising number of small but easily checkable factual errors.

Documentaries

There have been five documentaries on *The Hitchhiker's Guide to the Galaxy* and its creator. The first was *The Making of The Hitchhiker's Guide to the Galaxy*, described in Chapter Six.

In March 1998, the twentieth anniversary of the radio series was marked with a half-hour documentary on Radio 4, narrated by Peter Jones, *The Guide to Twenty Years' Hitchhiking*. This was subsequently released on cassette, accompanied by an unedited 40-minute interview, as *Douglas Adams' Guide to The Hitchhiker's Guide to the Galaxy*. Both the documentary and the interview were then incorporated into CD releases of the complete twelve-episode series. Another radio programme was *So Long, and Thanks for All the Fish*, a half-hour posthumous tribute to Douglas Adams, presented by Geoffrey Perkins in September 2001.

In the wake of Adams' death, the BBC commissioned a television documentary/tribute as part of the *Omnibus* strand, entitled *Douglas Adams – The Man Who Blew Up the Earth*. Broadcast in August 2001, the programme was the expected mix of talking heads and interview clips, all recounting the same stories. It was really produced too close to its subject's passing for any of the participants to be truly objective.

The Adams estate were said to be unhappy with the choice of participants in the *Omnibus* programme and commissioned their own documentary, *Life, the Universe and Douglas Adams*. This was slightly longer and featured different interviewees but told basically the same story. It was narrated by Neil Gaiman but marred slightly by a couple of captions carelessly mistranslating British colloquialisms. *Life, the Universe and Douglas Adams* played a few film festivals and was made available on VHS through douglasadams.com.

Neither documentary did more than skim the surface of Adams' life and career and both recounted anecdotes which have subsequently been shown to be untrue.

In addition to all the above, the DVD of the *Hitchhiker's Guide* movie includes a *Making of* documentary directed by Grant Gee.

9. The Hitchhiker's Guide to the Galaxy Overseas

USA

The Hitchhiker's Guide to the Galaxy first appeared across the Atlantic in 1980 as a hardback and was broadcast on National Public Radio shortly after, but few people noticed.

Pocket Books changed all this with an advert in *Rolling Stone* in August 1981, offering a free *Hitchhiker's Guide* paperback to the first 3,000 readers to write in, and shortly afterwards Douglas Adams flew to America to discuss with ABC the possibility of remaking the TV series as an American production. However, after a couple of meetings it was discovered that to make the first 22-minute episode to a standard that US audiences would expect would require a budget of $2.2 million. The idea was quickly dropped and never mentioned again.

By the time that Pocket Books published *The Restaurant at the End of the Universe* in October 1982, Adams' profile was big enough to make the bestseller charts. But it was *Life, the Universe and Everything* which caused problems.

'I think that what happened was that my US publisher

was unhappy about using the word "fuck" because of the number of kids who read the books,' explained Adams later. 'I was a bit frustrated by that, but then it gave me an idea and I put in the whole Belgium piece.'

The problem was the party scene, in Chapter 21 (Chapter 22 in the UK edition), featuring the Rory Award for 'Most Gratuitous Use of the Word "Fuck" in a Serious Screenplay'. Fortunately, in 'Fit the Tenth' Zaphod Beeblebrox had used the swear word 'Belgium' and The Book had explained how it was considered a terrible obscenity in most civilised parts of the galaxy. Douglas added this narration to the chapter and the publishers seemed happy with it.

There are other, less obvious changes: Wowbagger the Infinitely Prolonged, in the opening chapter (British version) tells Arthur Dent, 'You're a jerk, a complete asshole,' but in the American version 'asshole' has inexplicably become 'kneebiter' while the word 'shit' later in the book becomes 'swut'. When Ford and Arthur materialise at Lords, the line, 'In the crowd a man collapsed,' was deleted.

The Krikkit spaceship, in the British edition, appears with a noise like a hundred thousand people saying 'wop' which the Americans changed to 'whop,' presumably because, despite being used as a purely onomatopoeic term, the word might offend Italians. The chapter numbering in the two editions is also different: the British Chapter 3 is an unnumbered piece between chapters in the US edition, while Chapter 5 is missing altogether, and the Americans split Chapter 22 into three parts.

Interestingly, no such censorship was evident in the

American edition of *So Long, and Thanks for All the Fish*, which also uses the word 'fuck'. 'I think the book was so late they were just relieved to get it!' was Adams' explanation for this inconsistency.

The TV series finally made it to US screens in November 1982, the six episodes re-edited into seven half-hours. Trade journal *Variety* called it, 'an imaginative dud … an interesting comedic idea that didn't get anywhere [with] some clever animated graphics that were indecipherable on a regular-size set.' American videos and a laserdisc release appeared in 1993.

Simon Jones was sent out to America by the BBC to help publicise the series and found the American response very different to the British: 'I was ready to say, "Isn't it impressive? The BBC Special Effects Department working at full blast. Absolute cutting edge special effects," and the first thing the disc jockey said to me was, "Of course, what I liked about it especially was the deliberate tackiness of the effects." Quick shoe-shuffle, quick rethink, I said, "Yes, it was of course intentional."'

The United States has always led the way in publishing omnibus editions of the *Hitchhiker's Guide* novels, starting with *The Hitchhiker's Trilogy* in 1983. This was followed by *The Hitchhiker's Quartet* in 1986 (there was also a boxed set of paperbacks as *The Universe of Douglas Adams*). In 1989 *Young Zaphod Plays It Safe* and Douglas Adams' introductory *Guide to the Guide* were added to the volume, which was retitled *The More Than Complete Hitchhiker's Guide to the Galaxy*, followed by *The Ultimate Hitchhiker's Guide to the Galaxy* in 1996, including *Mostly Harmless*. Finally, an omnibus of the five novels without *Young Zaphod Plays It*

Safe or the *Guide to the Guide* appeared in 1999 as ... *The Hitchhiker's Trilogy*!

There have been two 'Tenth Anniversary' editions of *Hitchhiker's Guide* books – the first novel and the radio scripts – each of which included a new introduction by Douglas Adams. In 2004, the 25th anniversary of the book's publication was marked by two commemorative editions: a facsimile of the original US hardback and a large format book originally announced as the '25th Anniversary Deluxe Edition' but published as the '25th Anniversary Illustrated Edition'. This included several pages of photographs of rare and unusual *Hitchhiker's Guide* ephemera as well as a foreword by Terry Jones and a historical essay by MJ Simpson. Unfortunately, the demotion from 'deluxe' to 'illustrated' meant that all the photographs were black and white.

Germany

Per Anhalter Durch die Galaxis, the German edition of *The Hitchhiker's Guide to the Galaxy*, was the first ever translation of one of Adams' works when it was published in 1981. So popular was it that the Germans promptly went ahead and made their own radio series, *Per Anhalter Ins All*. This was adapted from the first six BBC scripts, but each episode in German ran to 50 minutes. The show proved enormously popular and was subsequently released on cassette and CD.

Per Anhalter Ins All (II) followed in 1991, a nine-part adaptation of the third and fourth books. Unfortunately, many of the principal cast were unavailable and the resulting series was unpopular with German fans. Much better was a five-part dramatisation of the novel of *Starship Titanic* in 1999.

All of Adams' works have been published in Germany, where *Mostly Harmless* is entitled *Einmal Rupert und Zuruck* ('Round trip to Rupert') and there are two different editions of *Dirk Gently's Holistic Detective Agency*: *Der Elektrische Monch* and *Dirk Gentlys Holistische Detektei*. There are German translations of *Last Chance to See* (book and CD-ROM), *The Deeper Meaning of Liff*, Neil Gaiman's *Don't Panic* and all three comic-book series. The TV series was dubbed into German in the early 1980s and has been released on video.

In 1994 Douglas Adams visited Germany to give readings which were released on CD as *Douglas Adams Live* but for reasons of international copyright are not available in Britain or America. An even stranger CD, also only released in Germany, is *At the End of the Universe – Homage a Douglas Adams*, an avant-garde jazz suite by Klaus Konig inspired by *Hitchhiker's Guide*.

France

All five *Hitchhiker's Guide* novels and both Dirk Gently adventures have been successfully published in France, and a 12-episode French radio series, a translation of the BBC scripts, was broadcast in 1995.

Uniquely, the French publisher of *Hitchhiker's Guide* also commissioned and published an A–Z encyclopaedia of the books, *Surtout Pas de Panique – Le Guide du Guide Galactique*, written and compiled by the series' translator, Jean Bonnefoy.

Finland

For such a small country, Finland has a remarkably active science fiction industry, and also produces a lot of radio drama. Not only have all of Adams' books been published in Finland, but Yleisradio have broadcast far more of his works than the BBC. Terry Pratchett, whose novel *Reaper Man* was adapted for Finnish radio, once commented, 'I get the impression that there's only three people in Finnish radio, but they're really great guys with a shitload of money, and they're having the time of their life doing whatever they want to do.'

The Finnish *Hitchhiker's Guide* was broadcast in 12 episodes in 1984, adapted from the BBC radio scripts; seven years later, *Life, the Universe and Everything* and *So Long, and Thanks for All the Fish* were adapted into a six-episode series featuring the same cast. Finland also enjoyed the only ever professionally dramatised Dirk Gently story, when *The Long Dark Teatime of the Soul* was broadcast in 18 episodes from December 1995. For reasons which are not entirely clear, although made in Finland and produced by the Finnish state broadcaster, all these productions were recorded and broadcast in Swedish.

Finland is one of three countries to have published a translation of *The Meaning of Liff* (Germany and the Netherlands are the other two), despite the fact that this is clearly impossible. However, Finland is unique in having not only translated the two existing *Liff* books but also published a third one.

Elsewhere

The Hitchhiker's Guide to the Galaxy has been translated into more than 30 languages, including French, Italian, German, Japanese, Ukrainian, Spanish, Portuguese, Hebrew, Greek, Dutch, Norwegian, Finnish, Hungarian and Polish. Many countries have also published *Last Chance to See*, *The Salmon of Doubt* and the two Dirk Gently novels.

In 1995, to celebrate the British hosting of the World Science Fiction Convention, the *Hitchhiker's Guide* Appreciation Society published a small pamphlet collecting numerous versions of Prostetnic Vogon Jeltz's poem, *Oh Freddled Gruntbuggly*, from foreign editions (and a few specially commissioned translations). It was entitled *A Young Vogon's Garden of Verse*.

10. The Film

Cast: Martin Freeman, Mos Def, Sam Rockwell, Zooey Deschanel, Bill Nighy, Alan Rickman, Warwick Davis, John Malkovich, Anna Chancellor, Richard Griffiths, Ian McNeice, Steve Pemberton, Helen Mirren

Story: Ford Prefect rescues his friend Arthur Dent from the destruction of Earth by hitching a lift with the Vogons. After suffering the captain's poetry, they are thrown off the ship but picked up by the *Heart of Gold*, which has been stolen by Zaphod Beeblebrox. Zaphod is on a quest, assisted by his half-human, half-alien girlfriend Trillian and Marvin the robot, to discover the great question of life, the universe and everything, to which the answer is 42. This quest takes the crew of the *Heart of Gold* to Viltvodle VI, where they meet the mad missionary Humma Kavula who takes Zaphod's second head as a hostage; to the bureaucratic hub of the galaxy, Vogsphere; and ultimately to the mighty supercomputer Deep Thought.

Background: The idea of a film version of *Hitchhiker's Guide* was discussed in print as early as 1979, but did not become a serious possibility until two years later, after the TV series had been and gone and with the second TV series definitely cancelled. By August 1982, Douglas Adams was telling interviewers, 'I think that there is now quite a good chance that there is soon going to be a film.'

In December 1982 it was announced that the film rights had been sold to Columbia Pictures and producer Ivan Reitman, with Adams contracted to write the screenplay and also acting as associate producer. A few months later, Adams was in Los Angeles, working on a script which was said to combine elements from all three published novels. Special effects expert Ron Cobb (*Alien*, *Star Trek II*) was attached to the project, and Columbia Pictures grandly (and somewhat naively) announced that the film would be released in 1985. Everything looked very promising, and the first draft of the screenplay was delivered in September 1983.

Adams and Reitman did not get on at all. After Adams' third draft he was dropped as writer and a further seven drafts were written by an experienced Hollywood scriptwriter named Abbie Bernstein, but by then Reitman was concentrating on a new project, *Ghostbusters*. Adams later claimed in interviews that Reitman had tried to change the Answer from 42 to something 'less disappointing', which was a great anecdote but not actually true.

By 1987 the project had faltered completely and the film went into limbo. Simon Jones very adroitly observed, 'I'm constantly amused by the progress of *Hitchhiker's Guide* from film company to film company, and figure that we'll all be drawing our pensions before it's actually made into a movie.'

In 1992, Douglas Adams bought back the film rights to

his own book from Columbia and by February 1994 he had completed a brand new first draft screenplay, to be shopped around to potential investors. His friend Mike Nesmith – ex-Monkee, inventor of MTV and head of Pacific Arts – was briefly attached as producer but things then went quiet again for a few years.

It was in January 1998 that *The Hitchhiker's Guide to the Galaxy* went back into active development, this time at Hollywood Pictures (through the labyrinthine process of Hollywood politics it was eventually released as a Spyglass Entertainment/Touchstone Pictures production). Jay Roach, who had sprung to prominence with the Austin Powers films, was attached as director and the project was shopped around the various studios for three years to no avail. The problem was that Adams, mindful of the Columbia farrago, had retained considerable control over the project, which put him at odds with any prospective studio: no one wanted to make his film and he would not allow anyone else to make theirs.

In May 2001 Roach decided to drop off the project but everything became moot that same month when Douglas Adams died suddenly. Tragic though this was, it shifted control of the project to the Adams estate who were more amenable to studio suggestions. A new American writer, Karey Kirkpatrick (*Chicken Run*) was assigned in late 2002 and, when his script was approved, the British pop video directing/producing team of 'Hammer and Tongs' (Garth Jennings and Nick Goldsmith) were brought aboard, with Roach staying on as a producer.

A wide range of interesting names were considered for the cast, including Hugh Grant and Ewan McGregor as

Arthur, and Jim Carrey and Robert Downey Jr as Zaphod. The movie was shot in Britain between April and August 2004 with aliens created by the Jim Henson Creature Shop. The casting of voice roles was left very late, with some of the key names only being confirmed less than three months before the April 2005 premiere. The narrator proved particularly difficult to cast, with both *Clangers* creator Oliver Postgate and veteran BBC wildlife presenter David Attenborough being considered before the role went to Adams' friend Stephen Fry.

Comment: In order to publish this edition of *The Pocket Essential Hitchhiker's Guide* around the same time that the movie is released, this section has been written without actually seeing the film itself. A test screening was held in Los Angeles in January 2005 from which several amateur reviews made it onto the web, mostly positive.

There was never going to be any serious possibility of the movie faithfully recreating the book, for two reasons. First, because the book is a picaresque adaptation of two-thirds of a six-part radio serial written week by week and as such is completely missing any sort of basic three-act structure. The second reason is that to do so would be untrue to the spirit of *Hitchhiker's Guide*. Until the mid-1980s, the franchise's distinctive feature was its refusal to stay true to itself as it spread across various media, a feature largely forgotten in the subsequent 20 years of sequels and literal adaptations. As executive producer Robbie Stamp (a friend and business partner of Douglas Adams) said: 'Every version of *Hitchhiker's* has been different and the movie is no different.'

The casting is mostly spot-on, although the choice of Stephen Fry as The Book is curious because, in Britain at least, this will sound like a celebrity narrator rather than the anonymous voice of an electronic travel guide. The design is also impressive: Marvin would be adorable if he only held himself properly and the Vogons (inspired by the caricatures of James Gillray) are suitably huge and ugly.

That said, there are two changes which may prove crucial, or at least controversial. In every other version, Zaphod's heads have been positioned side-by-side atop a Y-shaped spine. However, in the film the second head is underneath Zaphod's main head which tips back – the actor's beard becoming the prosthetic head's fringe – when the second head emerges. This head is also (somehow) detachable and Zaphod spends a considerable part of the film with only one head and two arms. More importantly, the second head has been given a character all of its own – Zaphod's libido – and a reason to exist: Presidents are only allowed half a brain so Zaphod hid the surgically removed 50 per cent in a concealed second head. This turns the reckless, feckless libertine of previous versions into an ersatz Jekyll and Hyde.

Most crucial of all, the central quest of the story has been altered. In all previous versions the narrative is driven by Arthur's desire for peace and quiet and a chance to return home, which becomes bound up with Zaphod's quest to steal the fabulous riches of semi-mythical Magrathea to finance a life of 'excitement and adventure and really wild things'. The search for the ultimate question to life, the universe and everything was a subplot, something which none of the main characters were really bothered about and in fact something which did not even concern our own universe. That, in a way, was what made the story so distinctive: the central characters considered finding a good cup of tea or a fun party more important than discovering the meaning of it all. This is, therefore, a sea-change and it remains to be seen how well the new story will work for the millions of people who have read and enjoyed the books, and indeed for the millions more encountering *Hitchhiker's Guide* for the first time on the big screen.

11. Dirk Gently

Dirk Gently's Holistic Detective Agency

Hardback: Heinemann, 1987
Paperback: Pan Books, 1988

Story: Richard MacDuff discovers, during the course of an incredibly complex adventure, that his tutor at Cambridge, Professor Urban Chronotis, Regius Professor of Chronology, is a time-travelling being. Together, the two of them prevent an evil alien entity from halting the Big Bang and thus causing the universe to not be created. They are assisted in this by an electronic monk, several versions of the Mona Lisa, an eccentric detective named Dirk Gently, and Samuel Taylor Coleridge.

Background: In early 1986, 18 months after the publication of *So Long, and Thanks for All the Fish*, came news that Douglas Adams was writing another novel – but it was nothing to do with *The Hitchhiker's Guide to the Galaxy*. It did, nevertheless, have a typically cumbersome Adams title: *Dirk Gently's Holistic Detective Agency*.

The hardback rights to the new book and a sequel were offered around and Douglas signed with Heinemann for

£575,000 and with Simon and Schuster (in the USA) for a staggering $2.27 million. And all this before a word had been written. Apparently.

Actually, quite a lot of the words in *Dirk Gently's Holistic Detective Agency* had already been written as Douglas went back to his *Doctor Who* scripts, *Shada* and *City of Death*, reusing elements of the storyline and replacing the Doctor with Dirk Gently.

The book was an immediate bestseller, promoted as 'a detective-ghost-horror-whodunnit-time-travel-romantic-epic'. It was also the first ever desk-top published novel, supplied as camera-ready copy direct from Adams' laser printer. 'It was a fascinating and therapeutic way of working,' claimed Adams, adding that the technique had shaved five weeks from the production schedule.

Comment: Response to Douglas Adams' first non-*Hitchhiker's Guide* novel was, on the whole, quite good. Critics and fans alike were generally agreed that it stood up on its own and was certainly comparable to Adams' earlier work. Douglas had proved that it was his name and talent that sold the novels, not the *Hitchhiker's Guide* branding.

Quite how many of these fans realised the extent to which *Dirk Gently's Holistic Detective Agency* borrowed from Adams' work for *Doctor Who* is not known – it was certainly unnoticed by the critics.

Dirk Gently's Holistic Detective Agency is entertaining, clever, witty and well-structured, but it has one enormous flaw. It is incredibly complicated, especially the ending, and few indeed are the people who have understood it after one reading, or even after several. Adams' tendency to allude to things without making them perfectly clear sometimes works (as with Elvis' cameo in *Mostly Harmless*) and sometimes misses completely (as with the original version of *Young Zaphod Plays It Safe*). The ending of *Dirk Gently's Holistic Detective Agency*, it must be said, is a miss, if not quite a mess. Adams himself subsequently admitted that even he could not completely follow what was going on in the final chapters.

The Long Dark Teatime of the Soul

Hardback: Heinemann, 1988
Paperback: Pan Books, 1989

Story: In his second adventure, Dirk Gently gets mixed up with a young lady named Kate Schecter and a range of ancient Norse gods who hang around St Pancras Station. The solution this time lies in something more prosaic than Coleridge's work – a pop record entitled *Hot Potato* is the key.

Background: *The Long Dark Teatime of the Soul* was another bestseller, establishing Dirk Gently as a franchise in its own right. This second outing for the character was actually slightly better than the first, possibly because it was a completely original story. Hopes were high for a third Dirk Gently book, but it never appeared (at least, not in a finished version).

In 1993, a paperback omnibus edition of both Dirk Gently novels was published, and a hardback omnibus edition appeared in the USA the following year. Professor Chronotis reappeared in a short story in a late 1990s *Doctor Who* annual. The story was uncredited, but was not by Douglas Adams.

Comment: Is *The Long Dark Teatime of the Soul* a better book than *Dirk Gently's Holistic Detective Agency*? Opinion is divided. It is certainly better at being a book, in that it was clearly conceived as a novel and wasn't stitched together from parts of used or unused TV scripts. It is also far less confusing than its predecessor and can even be understood on its first reading.

The main problem, which also affected the first book but less so, is that Dirk Gently himself has comparatively little to do. Adams has tremendous fun playing with ideas and characters, twisting them into a plot, and somewhere in there is Dirk Gently. But removing the character of Gently from the book would not harm it to any great extent.

That's the curious thing about Dirk Gently: he is a terrific idea and has proved himself, in his limited literary life, to be a popular character with readers. But his influence on his own novels is often minimal.

Nevertheless, *Long Dark Teatime* is that rarest of things – a Douglas Adams novel which stands on its own, works on its own, and can be read in isolation from his other works.

Dirk Gently on Tape

Given that there are only two books in the series, the history of Dirk Gently on audio tape is ridiculously complex.

The first talking book to appear was a two-tape abridged version of *Dirk Gently's Holistic Detective Agency*, read by the author, which was released by Hamlyn Books on Tape in 1988, and shortly afterwards in America by Simon and Schuster Audioworks. The following year, when *Long Dark Teatime* was published in paperback, Simon and Schuster Audioworks released a two-tape abridged reading of that book by Simon Jones.

Dove Audio released an unabridged reading, by the author, of *Long Dark Teatime* in 1991, and this was released in the UK in 1992 as part of the BBC Audio Collection, despite the fact that it had never been broadcast.

In 1997 Dove finally released an unabridged *Dirk Gently's Holistic Detective Agency*, read by the author but a different recording to the previous abridged version. This surfaced in Britain in 1998 on the Isis label, who had by then released all the Dove *Hitchhiker's Guide* readings. Finally, in late 1999, both unabridged readings were re-released in the United States by Dove as a single eight-tape pack.

Consequently, the two Dirk Gently books have spawned no fewer than eight releases of four readings on five record labels.

Dirk Gently on Screen

The one and only TV appearance of Dirk Gently was in *The South Bank Show* in January 1992. This was a strangely surreal programme featuring interaction between Douglas Adams' world and his fictional characters. Simon Jones and David Dixon recreated their roles from the TV series,

Peter Jones provided some narration, and Marvin put in an appearance (voiced by Stephen Moore), although he had to wear a long overcoat as the BBC could only find his head.

The South Bank Show also featured Dirk Gently, played by Michael Bywater, a friend of Adams whose best known work is probably the *Bargepole* column in *Punch*. Two other characters from *Dirk Gently's Holistic Detective Agency*, Richard MacDuff and the Electric Monk, were both played by Paul Shearer.

In 1995 Douglas Adams told an interviewer: 'There's a TV series in development at the moment based on Dirk Gently. I can't give you any dates other than to say that at this level of television just the contract took a year to write.'

The TV series never progressed beyond an initial idea – using the character but not the plot of either novel. However, a TV movie based on *Dirk Gently's Holistic Detective Agency* was mooted in 1996 and author Michael Marshall Smith was brought in to write the script. Smith was ex-Footlights, like Adams, and had been a huge fan of *Hitchhiker's Guide* in his younger days. After a spell writing comedy for TV and radio, Smith turned to fiction and picked up a slew of British and World Fantasy Awards.

'What's going to be the biggest challenge of dramatising Dirk Gently,' he mused, shortly after submitting a rough treatment of the script, 'is that the character of Dirk is a centre around which things happen. He's not an active character, he sort of pulls in the stuff. It's a writing conceit and that's why it works so well as text. The challenge is going to be dramatising that so that people understand.

What I don't want to do is turn it into a rubbish detective thing.' However, after a couple of meetings the project was dropped and has not resurfaced since.

Then, in early 2000, Douglas Adams announced that he himself had got as far as page five of a Dirk Gently feature film screenplay. Michael Nesmith, previously attached to the *Hitchhiker's Guide* movie, was named as producer but Adams emphasised that there was no way the Dirk Gently film would happen before the *Hitchhiker's Guide* one.

Dirk Gently on Stage

Like *The Hitchhiker's Guide to the Galaxy*, Dirk Gently has found the theatre stage easier to conquer than the cinema screen. A stage adaptation of the first novel, with its title conveniently shortened to *Dirk*, began life as a school production in 1991. According to the play's website, 'It was very short (about an hour), and by all accounts, amusing but utterly incomprehensible.'

In May 1995, a proper stage production of *Dirk* was presented in Oxford by a group of undergraduates. The script was written by Arvind David (who also directed) and James Goss and the play was produced by Matt Wreford. The show featured excellent costumes and props, professional-quality acting, and innovative computer graphics projected onto a screen above the stage. But what astounded audiences was the script which achieved the almost impossible task of making the plot comprehensible.

The play received glowing reviews and was praised by Douglas Adams, who attended the final performance.

'They managed to solve the problem of how you deal with lots of complexities and contradictions by simply ignoring them,' he commented. 'It was wonderful!'

A revival was staged at the Oxford Playhouse in November 1997, again to great acclaim. David and Goss rewrote the script, even more high-tech computer graphics sequences were included, Wreford returned as producer and the director was Alex Potts. With help from the National Theatre and the National Lottery, the production proved even better than before – people travelled all the way from America just to see it.

The Salmon of Doubt

Hardback: Macmillan, 2002
Paperback: Pan Books, 2003

Background: Between 1994 and his death in 2001, Douglas Adams was contracted to write a novel entitled *The Salmon of Doubt* which at various times was a third Dirk Gently book, a sixth *Hitchhiker's Guide* book or something completely new. He would occasionally scribble ideas for such a book but never seriously sat down to write it.

When Adams died, material from his computer hard drives (and fans' scrapbooks) was collected into a book entitled *The Salmon of Doubt: Hitchhiking the Galaxy One Last Time*. This included 11 chapters of a third Dirk Gently novel. The British edition of the book includes a foreword by Stephen Fry, the US edition has a foreword by Christopher Cerf.

Comment: *The Salmon of Doubt*, as published, is an eclectic mix of fiction, non-fiction, opinion and interviews, very obviously betraying the haste with which it was compiled in order to be published – for some reason – on the first anniversary of its author's death. Some of the material in the book is very enjoyable, some is inconsequential, but only one of the 30 or so items stands out as entirely unnecessary and ironically it is the title story.

Chapters from several different drafts have been edited together to form a rambling, disconnected story. Very little actually happens apart from Dirk Gently travelling to America and a rhinoceros charging through a Californian garden. The basic set-up involves a cat which is somehow missing its rear half. However, the brevity of the work (it is a fragment, and for the publicity to pretend that it is an unfinished novel is ridiculous) coupled with its haphazard construction mean that nothing is even explored, let alone resolved. It is a detective story which never even gets as far as the main character doing any serious detecting.

Worse than that, the prose is clumsy and betrays little of the author's acclaimed style. *The Salmon of Doubt* reads exactly like what it is: rough, first draft scribbles around a vague idea. It is a sad way to remember a popular author and would have been better left unpublished.

12. Other Work by Douglas Adams

Footlights

Douglas Adams attended Saint John's College, Cambridge University from 1971 to 1974, and while there was invited to join the legendary Footlights Club. Founded in 1883, Footlights had helped to launch the careers of such comedy giants as Peter Cook, John Cleese, Graham Chapman and the Goodies. Many of the *Hitchhiker's* personnel, including Simon Jones, Mark Wing-Davey, Geoffrey McGivern, John Lloyd and Joe Melia, were members of Footlights before or during Adams' tenure.

From 1972 onwards, Douglas Adams performed sketches and monologues at numerous 'smoking concerts', the late-night entertainments staged by Footlights members for their peers which served as try-outs for material for the main revue. Through these 'smokers' he became friends with two other undergraduates, Will Adams (no relation) and Martin Smith (later immortalised in *Hitchhiker's Guide* as, 'bloody Martin Smith from Croydon'). As Adams-Smith-Adams, the trio became a major writing and performing force in Footlights.

Douglas Adams appeared briefly in the 1972 Footlights

Revue, not on stage but in a filmed segment. In June 1973, as a reaction against not being chosen to perform in that year's revue, Adams–Smith–Adams staged their own independent revue, *Several Poor Players Strutting and Fretting*, the first of several such productions. By 1974, Adams–Smith–Adams were such a regular fixture in Footlights that they confidently expected to perform in that year's revue, *Chox*, especially as their material accounted for more than half of the script. In the end, however, only Martin Smith was picked for the cast, which also included Griffith Rhys Jones (*sic*), Geoff McGivern and Clive Anderson.

Highlights from *Chox* were broadcast on BBC1 in August and followed by a short-lived Radio 4 series, *Oh No It Isn't!*, produced by Simon Brett; Adams–Smith–Adams were credited as writers on both the TV broadcast and the radio shows.

Douglas Adams, Will Adams and Martin Smith all graduated from Cambridge in 1974, and two years later Douglas was approached by Footlights to direct the 1976 revue, *A Kick in the Stalls*. Douglas Adams was also credited in the programme as one of the revue's writers, with Will Adams and Martin Smith providing additional material.

The last ever appearance of Adams–Smith–Adams was a writing credit in a 1981 independent revue, *An Evening Without*, which was a hit on the Edinburgh Festival Fringe of that year. An incredibly rare LP of the show was also produced.

Monty Python/Graham Chapman

Douglas Adams was always an enormous fan of Monty Python, and the Python influence on *Hitchhiker's Guide* (especially in its early incarnations) is obvious. Through his work with Footlights at Cambridge, Adams was able to meet first John Cleese and later Graham Chapman, with whom he collaborated on various projects. The fourth and final series of *Monty Python's Flying Circus* was retitled *Monty Python* and was made without John Cleese. Consequently Chapman was at a bit of a loose end and seeking other collaborators, one of whom was Douglas Adams.

Adams appears very, very briefly and almost unrecognisably in two Monty Python sketches. He is one of the 'pepperpot ladies' in one sketch, and he is a surgeon in another. He also received a credit for additional material in the last TV episode ever, broadcast in December 1974, and on the album of *Monty Python and the Holy Grail* he receives a credit because part of the linking material between soundtrack clips includes a heavily revised sketch of his about Marilyn Monroe.

Chapman and Adams also collaborated on a 1977 episode of *Doctor on the Go* entitled 'For Your Own Good' and a one-off sketch show in 1976, *Out of the Trees*, featuring Simon Jones and Mark Wing-Davey. One sketch from this, *The Private Life of Genghis Khan*, was later reworked by Adams into a short story for *The Utterly Utterly Merry Comic Relief Christmas Book*.

Also of note is *Our Show for Ringo Starr*, an unproduced special for American TV written by Chapman and Adams as a vehicle for the ex-Beatle. This script was finally published in 1999 in a book called *OJRIL: The Completely Incomplete Graham Chapman* and proved to be an uneasy mix of Beatle-esque and Python-esque humour which would have needed a lot of rewrites (and a huge budget) to be broadcastable. Douglas Adams is also one of several listed co-authors of Chapman's surreal memoir, *A Liar's Autobiography* although his contribution is very small.

Doctor Who

'I remember when I was at school I wrote an episode of *Doctor Who* just for us to do on the tape recorder,' Douglas Adams told an interviewer in 1978. 'Daleks being powered by Rice Krispies is about all I remember.'

Always a big fan of the long-running series, Adams' first attempt at writing for *Doctor Who* was a spec script (i.e. unsolicited) submitted to the show in 1974. This now-lost script was notable only for the idea of the 'B' Ark, a means to rid the world of the useless third of its population who don't actually do anything; this idea was reused in *Our Show for Ringo Starr*, and finally saw the light of day as the Golgrafrinchan 'B' Ark in *Hitchhiker's Guide*.

The Pirate Planet:

Broadcast: September 1978

Cast: Tom Baker, Mary Tamm, John Leeson, Bruce Purchase, Andrew Robertson, Bernard Finch, David Sibley, Primi Townsend, David Warwick, Rosalind Lloyd
Director: Darrol Blake

In 1977, while waiting for BBC Radio to decide whether or not they wished to make a series of *Hitchhiker's Guide*, Adams submitted the pilot script for his series to the then script-editor of *Doctor Who*, Robert Holmes, as an example of his work. Holmes liked what he saw and commissioned a four-part story from Adams.

Broadcast as part of the six-story 'Key to Time' arc, *The Pirate Planet* concerned a hollowed-out world which transported itself through space, materialising around other planets and then stealing all their minerals and other material supplies. The cyborg captain of the planet even had an eye patch and a robotic parrot – this would not be the only time that a character created by Douglas Adams would wander around a TV series with a lifeless plastic thing attached to his shoulder.

To Douglas Adams' enormous surprise, Anthony Read (who had succeeded Holmes) asked him to take over as script editor on the show for the subsequent season (September 1979 to January 1980), during which Adams wrote two scripts.

City of Death:

Broadcast: September 1979

Cast: Tom Baker, Lalla Ward, Julian Glover, Catherine Schell, David Graham, Tom Chadbon, Kevin Flood
Director: Michael Hayes

City of Death concerned an alien whose attempts to prevent the explosion that destroyed him involved stealing the Mona Lisa. The Doctor's task was to ensure that the explosion actually happened, as it was directly responsible for the existence of life on Earth. John Cleese and Eleanor Bron made a memorable cameo appearance as a couple in an art gallery who mistake the TARDIS for a modern sculpture. This story actually began life as a script by David Fisher, but when it ran into problems, Adams and producer Graham Williams were called in to finish it under the pseudonym 'David Agnew'.

Shada:

Not broadcast

Cast: Tom Baker, Lalla Ward, David Brierley, Denis Carey, Christopher Neame, Victoria Burgoyne, Daniel Hill
Director: Pennant Roberts

Shada was a chase through space and time which concerned a retired Time Lord posing as a Cambridge Don under the name Professor Chronotis. This story achieved infamy because a BBC technician's strike prevented its completion, although footage was used in the 1983 adventure *The Five Doctors* to compensate for Tom Baker's unavailability. It was eventually released on video in 1992, complete with a copy of the script and with Tom Baker bridging the gaps in the footage. Douglas Adams' royalties from the video were donated to Comic Relief.

In 2003, *Shada* was remade as an audio production 'webcast' by the BBC and then released on CD. The story was slightly rewritten for the new medium and to cater for the casting of Paul McGann (the ninth Doctor) in place of Tom Baker.

The Pirate Planet, City of Death and *Shada* are among the very few *Doctor Who* stories never to have been novelised. There were plans to publish the scripts of *The Pirate Planet* in 1993, but after being postponed to 1994, the book was cancelled.

Doctor Who and the Krikkitmen:

Apart from the above, Douglas Adams wrote one other *Doctor Who* story as a film treatment, which was not only never made but never actually optioned for production. It concerned a race of evil, cricket-playing warrior robots attempting to save their home planet from the black hole to which it had been banished.

This storyline was eventually used for the third *Hitchhiker's* novel, with Slartibartfast as the Doctor and Arthur Dent replacing Sarah Jane Smith as the confused Earthling. Although the book claimed to be based on the later episodes of the radio series, it is essentially a noveli-sation of *Doctor Who and the Krikkitmen*.

The Meaning of Liff

Paperback: Pan Books/Faber & Faber, 1983
Hardback (revised): Pan Books, 1990
Paperback (revised): Pan Books, 1991

Background: *The Meaning of Liff* is most commonly described as a spoof dictionary. It is a collection of place names, each of which is given an amusing definition. As the introduction put it: 'There are many hundreds of common experiences, feelings, situations and even objects which we all know and recognise, but for which no words exist. On the other hand, the world is littered with thou-sands of spare words which spend their time doing nothing but loafing about on signposts pointing at places.'

The book began life as excerpts 'from *The Oxtail English Dictionary*' in the 1981 book *Not 1982*, and was published in its own right in 1983 as a small, stylish, black paperback. True to the definition of 'liff' – 'A book, the contents of which are totally belied by its cover. For instance, any book the dustjacket of which bears the words, "This book will change your life."' – the book carried a small orange sticker claiming, 'This book will change your life.'

An American edition was published in 1984 with some of the more Anglocentric definitions replaced or altered. The idea was revived in 1986 when a handful of addi-tional Liff definitions, by Adams, Lloyd and Stephen Fry, were included in *The Utterly Utterly Merry Comic Relief*

Christmas Book, and an expanded version of the original book, *The Deeper Meaning of Liff*, followed a few years later. There have even been foreign language versions in Germany, Finland and the Netherlands.

Comment: There is no doubt that *The Meaning of Liff*, co-written with John Lloyd, is one of the oddest entries in Douglas Adams' bibliography. It is also one of the funniest and, because if its bite-size structure, one of the most easily accessible.

It is very clear that Adams and Lloyd had tremendous fun with the book, not just in choosing the words and definitions, but in the overall layout. A series of maps becomes progressively sillier and less helpful, the letter K for example being a map of South America with every place name indicated as 'off the map' with the exception of the tiny Chilean island of Kent. The equally enjoyable index includes such great entries as 'darkness, groping for objects in,' 'things, various,' '*Wind, Gone with the*' and 'bddbbrrddrddrr, things that go.'

Last Chance to See

Hardback: Heinemann, 1990
Paperback: Pan Books, 1991
CD-ROM for Macintosh: 1995
CD-ROM for Windows: 1996

Background: In 1986, Douglas Adams was asked by *The Sunday Times* to travel to Madagascar and seek out the aye-

aye, a worryingly rare species of lemur. As well as writing his feature for the newspaper's colour supplement, Adams also turned the adventure into a programme for Radio 4.

Realising that he could use his celebrity to highlight his interest in ecology, Adams hatched a plan to repeat and expand the process, travelling around the world with zoologist Mark Carwardine in search of animals threatened with extinction. Originally announced for 1987, the trip eventually happened in 1989 and resulted in the book and radio series *Last Chance to See*.

Response to the book was enthusiastic, although as non-fiction it wasn't given as much media coverage as a new Douglas Adams novel would have been. Nevertheless it sold reasonably well and was extensively translated. There was even an abridged audiobook.

'It was a bit rough, I felt,' was Adams' view of the radio series, for which he and Carwardine had carried expensive recording equipment around the world. 'We were given minimal time for editing and production and the thing was rushed out without a lot of promo. I felt a little aggrieved by the whole thing, to be honest. They only paid Mark and me presenter's fees. Nothing for travel or expenses – we had to pay all of that. We even had to pay the expenses of the producer and the sound recordists. So the radio series left us tens of thousands of pounds out of pocket and without a good programme to show for it. I was less than happy.'

A second radio series of *Last Chance to See* in 1997 was simply readings, by Adams, from the book.

Computer games aside, Douglas Adams has only ever made one foray into the CD-ROM medium. *Last Chance to See* contained the entire text of the book, 800 photographs, an unabridged reading of the book by Adams plus additional narration recorded especially for the CD-ROM, and an hour of extracts from the radio series.

Comment: When asked about his favourite among his own books, Douglas Adams invariably pointed to *Last Chance to See*, and this is an opinion shared by many of his readers. What seems to have happened is that, after years of writing about bizarre alien creatures on exotic planets, Adams realised that even weirder creatures inhabit the far-flung corners of the Earth, and that somebody should bring them to the human race's attention while they're still here.

The kakapo, for example, is an idea that would have fitted in on any of the extraterrestrial worlds described in (and by) *The Hitchhiker's Guide to the Galaxy*: a flightless parrot whose decline in numbers is blamed by naturalists on the observation that the male kakapo's mating call actually repels the female.

Adams' interest in ecology continued to the end of his life. He was a patron of Save the Rhino International and the Dian Fossey Gorilla Fund and both charities now benefit from funds raised by the annual Douglas Adams Memorial Lecture.

Doctor Snuggles

One of the most unlikely credits on Douglas Adams' CV is *Doctor Snuggles*, a Dutch cartoon series about a bumbling but happy inventor who had adventures with his friends while building devices to make the world a better place. Filled with talking trees and happy badgers, it was designed to be the world's first non-violent TV cartoon, and was as twee as animation can get. Adams and John Lloyd wrote two episodes. Peter Ustinov voiced the main character.

'My recollection is pretty dim at this point,' admitted Adams, many years later, 'but I remember we came up with one episode about a river that was hiding in a cave because someone was stealing chunks of the ocean. I can't remember what the other one was about. It was just a job for a couple of hungry wannabes, but I do recall that we had a lot of fun doing it. I never managed to see the actual programme, so I don't know how they turned out, but I believe that one of them won some awards (which we also never saw, of course ...).'

Other Radio and Television Work

Although Douglas Adams never wrote for the TV series *Not the Nine O'Clock News* (produced by John Lloyd), he is listed among the contributors to three spin-off books: *Not! The Nine O'Clock News*, *Not 1982* and *Not 1983*. The only element of these books which is very clearly by Adams is a series of spoof word definitions scattered throughout *Not 1982*. Most of these turned up, some slightly amended, in *The Meaning of Liff*.

On radio, Douglas Adams made occasional contributions to *Week Ending* and *The Burkiss Way*, which in later episodes lampooned him mercilessly. In December 1978, he produced Radio 4's pantomime, *Black Cinderella II*

Goes East, which featured a cast drawn entirely from ex-Footlights' personnel. Subsequent forays into radio by Douglas Adams have included the natural history programme *Last Chance to See*, a half-hour tribute to the late Peter Jones, and two short series on new technology.

Apart from *The Hitchhiker's Guide to the Galaxy*, Douglas Adams has only ever created one actual TV programme, which was a one-off, hour-long 1990 BBC production called *Hyperland*. In this dramatised look at information technology, Adams (as himself) fell asleep in front of the television and was guided through his dreams by a 'software agent' played by Tom Baker.

Hyperland was broadcast before anybody had heard of the World Wide Web, and in retrospect looks incredibly prophetic, although Adams was wrong as much as he was right. Nevertheless, as probably the last serious attempt to present a popular science view of where communication technology could lead to before it actually got up and went there, the programme is of enormous historical interest.

13. The Digital Village

In 1994, Douglas Adams made a quantum leap from writing scripts and novels when he co-founded The Digital Village (TDV), along with Robbie Stamp and Richard Creasey, both former executives with Central Television. Despite the enormous cumulative business experience of the various TDV board members, it was Douglas Adams as 'Chief Imagineer' who was very much the public face of the company.

Initially, The Digital Village was just a website, www.tdv.com, which did little more than publicise The Digital Village. All manner of potential projects were mooted, including TV series, books, films, CD-ROMs, websites and other media not even dreamt of yet.

The first product to appear from The Digital Village was *Starship Titanic*.

Starship Titanic – The Game

Background: *Starship Titanic* was to be Douglas Adams' second great franchise. The concept actually began life as a throwaway joke in *Life, the Universe and Everything*, referring to a fabulous interstellar liner which underwent Spontaneous Massive Existence Failure. Indeed, the title

149

was briefly considered as being used for another *Hitchhiker's Guide* book.

However, with the establishment of TDV, Adams re-imagined *Starship Titanic* as a combined game and novel franchise, possibly also leading to a movie. The idea was that, rather than a computer game based on a book (as the *Hitchhiker's Guide* game had been in the 1980s) or a novel-isation of a computer game, the two would be developed in parallel.

Adams had professed great admiration for the popular adventure game *Myst* and wanted *Starship Titanic* to look equally gorgeous. To this end, he enlisted the help of designers Oscar Chichoni and Isabel Molina, known for their work on the film *Restoration* who between them created a quite stunningly designed spacecraft, with a canal (complete with robotic gondoliers) running the entire length of the ship. A state-of-the-art text parser was also incorporated in order to make conversations with the robots which staffed the ship as realistic as possible.

Unfortunately, like almost everything else on Douglas Adams' CV, *Starship Titanic* (released in association with Simon and Schuster Interactive) didn't appear on time. The game was officially launched in June 1997 at the E3 computer games conference in Atlanta, and it was hoped to be commercially available later that year, but was put back to January 1998 and finally released in April of that year, thus missing the important Christmas market.

Press build-up had been very positive, with computer magazines cooing over the stunning designs and expecta-tions high for entertainment value because of Adams' involvement (although he was not the sole writer).

However, hesitant rescheduling of the launch, combined with the non-availability of review copies and technical problems with the few copies that were released in advance, severely dented the game's launch.

It did not help that the game was only available for PC, and the Macintosh version, first shown off at the Apple Expo in November 1998, did not appear until March 1999, nearly a year after the PC game. Given Douglas Adams' known preference for Macs, this surprised many people, although he explained that the staggered release was more due to commercial demands than technical ones, and anyway it allowed the Mac version to be more thoroughly tested.

Comment: When reviewers finally had the chance to actually play the game, critical response was very mixed. The most frequent complaint was that, though the puzzles were wacky and potentially entertaining, many of the solutions were simply arbitrary and could not be arrived at by any means other than constant trial and error. Furthermore the widely scattered elements of the game required a lot of very long and tedious travel around the ship for each attempt.

The characters sadly failed to capture the public's imagination, even the manic parrot which was voiced by Terry Jones. In fact there were two Pythons featured in the game; 'Kim Bread,' the actor playing the talking bomb, was swiftly discovered to be John Cleese. When questioned about this, Adams' straight-faced response was, 'I've never heard of this Cleese person you mention.'

Although it did win the Software and Information

Industry Association's 1998 'Codie' award for 'Best New Adventure/Role Playing Software Game,' the overall response to *Starship Titanic* was disappointing and clearly less than the game's creators were hoping for.

Starship Titanic – The Novel

Paperback: Pan Books, 1997

Story: The *Starship Titanic* is the most incredible spaceship ever built, but cost-cutting measures mean that immediately after launch it undergoes Spontaneous Massive Existence Failure. It lands on Earth, where three friends board it for no apparent reason and are whisked off into the cosmos.

Classified as the lowest class of traveller, they must overcome a series of obstacles, including upgrading themselves, dealing with the many robots who operate the ship, coping with a manic parrot and defusing a talking bomb.

Background: Although it was technically entitled *Douglas Adams' Starship Titanic*, with Terry Jones credited as sole author, Adams and Jones were keen to stress in interviews that this was actually a collaborative work – but a serial, rather than parallel, collaboration. In other words, it was a novel by Jones based on a story by Adams.

With the delays undergone by the game, the novel should have had plenty of time to be written, but for various reasons which cannot be explored here it was actually left until the last moment. Adams and Jones had known each other since the days of the Monty Python TV series, and Jones was actually the first name ever rumoured as director of a *Hitchhiker's Guide* movie. The only previous direct collaboration between the two was the short story *A Christmas Fairly Story* in the 1986 *Comic Relief Christmas Book* which Adams had co-edited.

Although the American first edition was a hardback, the UK edition was a paperback original. This, combined with minimal point-of-sale material and the delay in the book's release, resulted in the title slipping out almost unnoticed, and it failed to make the book charts. Given the following of the two names on the cover, and that all of Adams' previous books – even *The Meaning of Liff* – had been bestsellers, this was a major disappointment. A strategy guide to the game was also published and there was a short-lived offer, via the website, of a collection of items (shower-cap, matchbook, etc.) such as might be found on the starship itself.

Comment: Given that this was Jones' first proper novel, and given the tremendous time constraints, it is no surprise that this book is frankly not very good. Critical response to the novel was lukewarm to say the least, with the general observation being that it read like somebody trying to write in Douglas Adams' style and not quite succeeding.

Even though it managed to be published in time for Christmas 1997, when the game should have been released but wasn't, the book still managed to be a few weeks late, due to difficulties with getting the UK proofs approved while Jones and Adams were touring the USA to sign copies of the American version. The first British edition actually had a terrible formatting problem in the introduction which left several pages with only one or two lines on them.

However, *Starship Titanic* was a genuine success in one part of the world. The German version, *Raumschiff Titanic*, was a big hit as both game and book (on which, it was very noticeable, the writing credit was 'Douglas Adams und Terry Jones'). There was even a German radio serial based on the novel, subsequently released on CD. But outside of Germany, *Starship Titanic* failed to leave the lasting mark on the games market the way its creators had hoped it would.

h2g2

Undaunted, the brains behind TDV prepared for their second venture, *h2g2*. Since the early days of the company, Adams had talked about producing some sort of Internet search engine, capitalising on the recognisability of the *Hitchhiker's Guide to the Galaxy* name as a branding tool. What was known until 1998 as *The Hitchhiker's Guide to the Internet*, was finally launched live on *Tomorrow's World* in April 1999, under the name *h2g2*.

h2g2 is described as a 'global Internet community' and has the lofty ambition of effectively recreating *The Hitchhiker's Guide to the Galaxy* for real. Since its launch, a worldwide army of thousands of 'researchers' have contributed information on every subject under the sun, with a team of editors helping to sort and either accept or reject submissions. Though the database thus created continues to grow at an alarming rate, the sheer scale of the project means that it will be some time before it can become the prime repository of knowledge which its creators hope.

TDV collapsed in late 2000 but *h2g2* was rescued by the BBC, where it was relaunched a few weeks before Douglas Adams' death and where it still survives.

Apart from *h2g2* and *Starship Titanic*, TDV's other products were scanty. Through its website it sold signed copies of *The Illustrated Hitchhiker's Guide to the Galaxy*, and a video of Douglas Adams reading extracts from the *Hitchhiker's Guide* novels (recorded in Islington in 1995 and previously available in America in both audio and video forms). The company also released an album by guitarist Robbie McIntosh and was credited as production company on Adams' two Radio 4 series on information technology, *The Internet: The Last Twentieth Century Battleground* and *The Hitchhiker's Guide to the Future*.

When Douglas Adams invented the idea of *The Hitchhiker's Guide to the Galaxy*, a hand-held, electronic repository of all knowledge, the idea was science fiction – and satirical science fiction at that. As a story, *Hitchhiker's Guide* was never meant to be prophetic in any way. But with the advent of WAP technology making *h2g2* available through mobile phones, such a device does now actually exist.

There is something wonderfully ironic in the fact that it took less time for technology to turn *The Hitchhiker's Guide to the Galaxy* into reality than for Hollywood to turn it into a film ...

14. The Hitchhiker's Guide to the Galaxy on the Web

The range of *Hitchhiker's Guide* material available on the web has changed completely since the first edition of this book in 2001. Both Douglas Adams' official site at **www.douglasadams.com** and the *Floor 42* fansite at **www.floor42.com** pretty much ceased to operate as going concerns when Douglas died in May 2001, although both still exist as archives.

There are now three main sites: *Planet Magrathea* at **www.planetmagrathea.com** is this author's own news site, updated daily with all the latest on Adams and *Hitchhiker's Guide*; the *Douglas Adams Continuum* at **www.douglasadams.se** has an active discussion forum; and the *Douglas Adams Portal* at **www.douglasadams. info** is the entrance to a network of sites featuring several exclusive interviews. There is also an active newsgroup at **alt.fan.douglas-adams**.

All these sites are in English, but there are also excellent sites run by fans in Japan (**home.u08.itscom.net/ hedgehog**), Poland (**www.nie-panikuj.w.pl**) and Brazil (**www.milliways-brasil.net**).

ZZ9 Plural Z Alpha is the Official *Hitchhiker's Guide to the Galaxy* Fan Club, a fan-run organisation which was founded in 1980 and produces a quarterly magazine, *Mostly Harmless* (first published 12 years before the novel of that name). A friendly, sociable and on occasions downright silly club, ZZ9 also offers a range of members-only merchandise and holds meetings around the country. The ZZ9 website is at **www.zz9.org**, or you can write for membership information, enclosing an SAE, to: 4 The Sycamores, Hadfield, Glossop, Derbyshire SK13 2BS, UK.

The official website for the *Hitchhiker's Guide* movie is **www.hitchhikersmovie.com**, while the 25th anniversary edition of the novel is served by an interesting site at **www.42words.com**. The BBC has three excellent sites about the original radio series (**www.bbc.co.uk/bbc7/drama/progpages/hitchhikers.shtml**), the new radio series (**www.bbc.co.uk/radio4/hitchhikers**) and *Hitchhiker's Guide* in general (**www.bbc.co.uk/cult/hitchhikers**).

Douglas Adams was a patron of The Dian Fossey Gorilla Fund (**www.gorillas.org**) and Save the Rhino International (**www.savetherhino.com**), both excellent charities which deserve your support.

Douglas Adams – A Select Bibliography

Books by Douglas Adams
The Hitchhiker's Guide to the Galaxy (1979)
The Restaurant at the End of the Universe (1980)
Life, the Universe and Everything (1982)
The Meaning of Liff (with John Lloyd, 1983)
So Long, and Thanks for All the Fish (1984)
The Hitchhiker's Guide to the Galaxy: The Original
   Radio Scripts (1985, revised in 2003)
Dirk Gently's Holistic Detective Agency (1987)
The Long Dark Teatime of the Soul (1988)
Last Chance to See (with Mark Carwardine, 1990)
The Deeper Meaning of Liff (with John Lloyd, 1990)
Mostly Harmless (1992)
The Illustrated Hitchhiker's Guide to the Galaxy (1994)
The Salmon of Doubt (2002)
The Hitchhiker's Guide to the Galaxy: 25th Aniversary
   Illustrated Edition (2004)

Other Douglas Adams–related books
A Liar's Autobiography (by Graham Chapman, 1980)
Not! The Nine O'Clock News (1980)
Not 1982 (1981)
Not 1983 (1982)

The Utterly Utterly Merry Comic Relief Christmas Book (ed. Douglas Adams and Peter Fincham, 1986)

Living in Words: Interviews from The Bloomsbury Review (1988)

The Utterly Utterly Amusing and Pretty Damn Definitive Comic Relief Revue Book (1989)

Don't Panic (by Neil Gaiman, 1988)

Hockney's Alphabet (ed. Stephen Spender, 1991)

Wordsmiths of Wonder (by Stan Nicholls, 1993)

Animal Passions (ed. Alan Coren, 1994)

The Great Ape Project (ed. Paolo Cavalieri and Peter Singer, 1994)

The Wizards of Odd (ed. Peter Haining, 1996)

Douglas Adams' Starship Titanic (by Terry Jones, 1998)

Douglas Adams' Starship Titanic: The Official Strategy Guide (by Neil Richards, 1998)

Monty Python Speaks! (by David Morgan, 1999)

OJRIL: The Completely Incomplete Graham Chapman (ed. Jim Yoakum, 1999)

The Pocket Essential Hitchhiker's Guide (by MJ Simpson, 2001)

Digging Holes in Popular Culture (ed. Mike Russell, 2001)

Hitchhiker: A Biography of Douglas Adams (by MJ Simpson, 2003)

The Book of the Future (2003)

Wish You Were Here: The Official Biography of Douglas Adams (by Nick Webb, 2003)

Don't Panic! Essays on British TV SF (ed. John Cook, 2005)

The Making of The Hitchhiker's Guide to the Galaxy (ed. Robbie Stamp, 2005)

The Anthology at the End of the Universe (ed. Glenn Yeffeth, 2005)
The Science of The Hitchhiker's Guide to the Galaxy (by Michael Hanlon, 2005)

This select bibliography does not include reprints, omnibuses, audiobooks, US editions, translations, CD-ROMs or magazine articles – because if it did, it would take up this whole damn book!